PEOPLE LO♥E YOU

PEOPLE

THE REAL SECRET TO DELIVERING

LO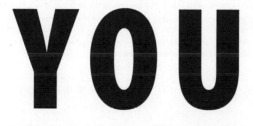E

LEGENDARY CUSTOMER EXPERIENCES

YOU

JEB BLOUNT

WILEY

John Wiley & Sons, Inc.

Published by John Wiley & Sons, Inc., Hoboken, New Jersey
Published simultaneously in Canada

For general information about our other products and services, please contact our Customer Care
Department within the United States at (800) 762-2974, outside the United States at (317) 572-3993 or
fax (317) 572-4002.

Wiley publishes in a variety of print and electronic formats and by print-on-demand. Some
material included with standard print versions of this book may not be included in e-books or in
print-on-demand. If this book refers to media such as a CD or DVD that is not included in the
version you purchased, you may download this material at http://booksupport.wiley.com. For more
information about Wiley products, visit www.wiley.com.

Library of Congress Cataloging-in-Publication Data:
Blount, Jeb.
    People love you: the real secret to delivering legendary customer experiences/Jeb Blount.
        pages   cm
    Includes index.
    ISBN 978-1-118-43324-9 (hbk. : alk. paper); ISBN 978-1-118-55587-3 (ebk);
ISBN 978-1-118-55588-0 (ebk); ISBN 978-1-118-55582-8 (ebk)
    1. Customer services.   2. Customer relations.   I. Title.
    HF5415.5.B56 2013
    658.8'12—dc23

                                                                            2012041952

Printed in the United States of America.

10 9 8 7 6 5 4 3 2 1

For Mom and Dee

Contents

About the Author

Jeb Blount is a leading expert on how human relationships impact account management, customer service, leadership and sales. He helps many of the world's leading organizations accelerate revenue growth and profits through focus on interpersonal relationships.

Jeb is the author of six books, including *People Buy You: The Real Secret to What Matters Most in Business; People Follow You: The Real Secret to What Matters Most in Leadership;* and *Power Principles.* He has published over 100 articles on account management, leadership and sales and his audio programs have been downloaded more than 6 million times on iTunes. More than 200,000 business professionals subscribe to his weekly newsletter.

As a business leader Jeb has more than 25 years of leadership experience and has served as a senior executive with Fortune 500s, SMBs and start-ups. In 2006, Jeb founded SalesGravy.com. Under Jeb's leadership Sales Gravy has experienced triple digit growth and today SalesGravy.com is the world's leading sales employment website, helping more than 7000 employers hire better salespeople fast.

Today Jeb spends much of his time on-site with his clients training leaders how to transform their organizations, drive change and improve performance by first improving human relationships with communication, coaching, sales process, and account management and customer service strategies.

To engage Jeb to speak to your team or group contact carrie@salesgravy.com or call Carrie Martinez at 706-664-0810 x102. To contact Jeb write to jeb@salesgravy.com, Twitter @ salesgravy or connect on LinkedIn, Facebook, or Sales Gravy. Visit www.JebBlount.com and www.PeopleBuyYou.com to learn more about our unique training programs and how we can help you and your company deliver legendary customer experiences.

1 | What's Love Got to Do with It

As I boarded the 737, I looked longingly at the folks who were comfortably ensconced in their large, leather, first-class seats, sipping on pre-flight drinks. I glanced again at the seat assignment on the boarding pass in my hand, reminding myself that I could do anything for two hours.

I routinely fly more than 100,000 miles a year. Because of the time I spend in airports, and in the air, most people would never guess that I am terribly claustrophobic. I want to sit in an aisle seat, preferably in an exit row or in first class, where there is plenty of room and I can get up easily. I'm so claustrophobic that in most circumstances if I cannot get an aisle seat I will cancel and rebook my flight—even if it means I get home a day or two later.

Today I had no choice. One of my clients, who was having issues with revenue growth, was preparing for an important board meeting and needed my help with developing a strategic plan to get him out of the hole. He'd called the day before to say that all of the company's executives would be at a meeting in the corporate office the next day, and he wanted me there in person.

I'd booked my flight at the last minute—grabbing the last available seat on the plane. But that meant that I would be spending the next two hours sitting in what I considered the seat from hell—the very last row on the plane, right next to the window. I just prayed that the two people sitting next to me would be small people so I wouldn't feel so trapped. I'd begged for another seat when I arrived at the airport but the flight was full. So, I decided to make the best of it. I put a grin on my face; I had a book, my iPod, a snack, and a bottle of water. I could do this.

When I reached the back of the plane, I smiled at the flight attendant who was standing between the two restroom doors, watching the plane slowly fill to capacity, and reminding customers to place only one bag in the overhead storage compartment. I said, "Hi, how are you doing?"

She looked back at me with a scowl on her face, and said nothing.

I responded with a more caring tone of voice, "Having a bad day?"

To that she responded, scowl and all, "Every day here is a bad day!"

I got the message loud and clear: Shut up and leave me alone. I hate my job. I hate this company. And I hate passengers.

So I squeezed into the small seat, stuffed into the back corner of an already cramped airplane, and prayed that I would make it through the ordeal without being dragged off the plane in a strait-jacket while news reporters explained to the cameras how a business man had gone nuts, forcing an emergency landing. As the two biggest people I've ever seen sat down next to me, my chest felt crushed with anxiety; the straitjacket seemed like an increasingly real possibility.

The conversation I'd had with the flight attendant continued to play in my head over and over again, like a recording on a loop (perhaps a good thing because it kept my mind off of my plight). The flight was pure misery. Not just because of my claustrophobia but because the entire flight crew seemed to be, well . . . *mean*. They barked orders at grown men and women. They did not smile. Overall, they were unpleasant.

On the cab ride to my client's office, that same scene continued to play. All I could think about was how horrible the entire experience had been. But it was the words *"Every day here is a bad day!"* that kept ringing in my ears. The trip home was not as bad but I still couldn't let my encounter with that flight attendant go. I paid $1,200 to get on that flight. Twelve hundred dollars, to be treated like dirt! The more I thought about it, the more it disturbed me, and the more worked up I became. So I asked my company controller to pull a report of how much I'd spent with that particular airline over the previous six months.

Almost $50,000! She also pointed out that we spent more with this airline than any of our other vendors, except one. It was a big number and it felt personal. I'm a small business and that $50k is my money. Unlike the typical corporate traveler with an expense account and a corporate travel department, this money came out of my back pocket. Right then and there I resolved that I would never do business with this airline again, even if it cost more to fly with other airlines, unless there was absolutely no other choice.

Breaking up was hard to do, though. This airline generally had lower fares and more flights from my city. I had preferred status with the airline, so on any new airline I would have to start all over—meaning waiting in lines and getting bad seats. But I was resolved to see my boycott through. It has been a year since that incident, and though in some cases it has been inconvenient on my end, they have not received another dime from me.

The Case for Managing Customer Experience

My illustration above, something to which most people who have the occasion to travel can relate, is an example of how influential *experience* is on buying decisions. It is a reality check. Every touch point, every time you or someone in your company engages a customer, it creates an experience, something they remember. When people have positive emotional experiences, it anchors them to your brand, your product or service, and to *you*. When they have a negative experience, they tend to vote with their feet and their wallets and head straight to your competitors.

The focus on delivering great customer experiences is not new. Walt Disney, for example, made experience the foundation of Disneyland. For him Disneyland was a stage and the employees its cast members. His drive was to deliver an experience so powerful the memory lasted a lifetime. I have those memories and it is likely you do, too. It is this focus on experience that has kept Disneyland and Disney World from looking the same as their myriad competitors to consumers. While Disney's competitors have more thrilling, high-tech rides (trust me, I'm a theme park junkie), Disney creates an emotional connection with its patrons that is unparalleled.

In the late 1990s, a movement toward customer experience began in earnest. Dozens of books were written, studies were commissioned, and academics from Harvard and other well-known institutions began writing papers on the value of customer experience. They citied great business-to-consumer (B2C) companies like Disney, the Ritz Carlton, Rain Forest Café, and Nordstrom, among other well-known brands. Over the last decade, we have witnessed a new generation of companies including Amazon, Apple, Starbucks, and Zappos, all of whom embrace customer experience as a core business focus.

Today, the customer experience drum beats louder. The emergence and amalgamation of social media and technology that keeps us online and in touch 24 hours a day has created an environment unique in human experience. We live in the age of transparency. Customers have the ability to find anything about you, your product, service, company, and competitors in an instant, with minimal effort. Often they know more about your products and services than you do. Additionally, to the consternation of many business leaders, they have the ability to easily tell others how they feel about their experience with you through many social channels.

At the same time, people are quite literally overwhelmed with information. Smart phones, smart TVs, tablets, laptops, cars, and even smart refrigerators stream data from millions of sites and channels in an unending 24/7/365 flow of information. In this environment, people have become numb to advertising and traditional marketing. In the age of transparency, their trust in traditional advertising messages has waned while their trust in the opinions of friends, bloggers, and online comments and postings of those they consider reliable sources of influence has increased.

This has put advocacy, referrals, and personal recommendations on a new pedestal of importance. Gaining customers and growing your business through referrals is the least expensive marketing channel there is. Prospects and customers who come to you through referrals are more qualified, more likely to buy, and more likely to stick around for the long-term. This is not news to anyone. Referrals have always been an important source of leads. What is important to understand though, is that fewer leads will come to you and your business from traditional outbound marketing and advertising in the future, and more will come via recommendations from customers who become your advocates.

Customer experience is the marketing channel of the future. In fact, a 2009 study conducted by the Strativity Group, http://www.strativity.com indicated that companies that invested in customer experience management reported higher customer referral rates. Customers will and do expect more from their interactions with you and your company. However, they will readily advocate for you and recommend you to others when you deliver a memorable emotional experience.

How Customer Experience Management Applies to Business-to-Business Relationships

The vast majority of focus on customer experience, including studies, reports, books, and course work, is centered on business-to-consumer (B2C) environments. The authors, consultants, and scholars who produce these works do give cursory mention of the impact of customer experience in the business-to-business (B2B) environment, yet they rarely follow through with much detail. They seem uncomfortable addressing customer experience as it relates to business-to-business relationships. Likewise, most investment in customer experience management at the corporate level has come from B2C companies.

It makes sense. It is much easier to draw a straight line between, say, your experience staying at a Marriot Resort and your propensity to spend more money, become a repeat customer, and tell your friends, and the investment by Marriot to make that happen. That linkage is much harder to make if you are a company selling mundane industrial products to the oil and gas industry or providing document management services or uniform rental programs. When the phrase *customer experience* is mentioned to corporate executives running B2B companies, it is not uncommon to see eyes roll. This happens partly because the concept of customer experience and the process for managing customer experience is tied so directly to the B2C marketplace. B2B executives have a hard time seeing how the strategies used to deliver customer experience in the B2C environment relate to them and rightly so. There is a difference, and should B2B companies attempt to stage customer experience using the same methodology as Disney, they will fail and waste a lot of money doing so. For this reason customer experience as a concept is rightly met with skepticism in the B2B marketplace.

Business-to-business relationships are different and often far more complex than consumer-based relationships. For instance, most buyers in B2B relationships are not spending their own money, unless of course you are dealing with the business owner. B2B relationships may involve large sums of money, contractual agreements, strategic relationships, layers of influencers and end users. Relationships also tend to be long-term rather than transactional.

However, the one thing that skeptical B2B leaders ignore is that in B2B relationships, *customers are still people*: emotional, irrational humans who make buying decisions based on emotion, not companies, departments, org-charts or CSI scores. People. Penske understood this concept, for example, when they implemented *Ready Line Excellence* in response to the number one complaint of the people who use their rental trucks (businesses and consumers alike). "People don't like dirty trucks. It is something they get very emotional about," one executive told me. So Penske implemented a system wide focus on ensuring that every truck was clean and crisp looking before the keys were handed to the driver. This simple focus on emotional experience cost little to implement, yet is paying dividends (reflected in improved CSI scores and repeat business) because the focus is on how people experience Penske at the emotional level.

Colin Shaw, author of *The DNA of Customer Experience: How Emotions Drive Value* (Palgrave MacMillan, 2007) and a world thought leader on customer experience, points out, "A Customer Experience is about a number of things. It is about a physical Customer Experience, such as price, product, locations, opening times, and the channel that is used—that is stores, online, telephone, the features of the product, so on. Critically it is also about emotions—how a customer feels." Shaw's research indicates "that over 50 percent of a Customer Experience is *about emotions.*" As humans emotions drive virtually all of our behavior and cause us to *act*. Yet, as Shaw aptly states, businesses have largely ignored human emotion in the buying equation.

The concept of delivering a great customer experience is simple and intuitively we all know it makes sense because, of course, we are all customers. As a customer, when you feel happy, important, cared for, and respected you have a tendency to buy more and tell other people about your experience. But for some reason, as soon as we put our B2B hat on, we abandon what we know to be true and ignore human emotion in our business relationships. This is one of the reasons companies continue to delude themselves with customer satisfaction indexes and drone on and on about customer loyalty rather than focus on improving the emotional experiences of their customers.

There Is No Loyalty When Everything Looks the Same

Was I satisfied with my flight to Chicago? Yes. I left on time, arrived on time with my bags, and did so in one piece. That is what the airline promised when I purchased the ticket. Did I quit doing business with them? Yes.

My bet is you can easily recall similar experiences with companies you do business with, and you've either been tempted to never spend another dime with them again or actually done so. I'll also lay my book royalties on the line and bet that each of those businesses has a slogan, motto, saying, or written document that proclaims something along the lines of "your complete satisfaction" or that "exceeding your expectations" is their goal. Internally, these same organizations likely spew propaganda to their employees admonishing that the goal is to create loyal customers.

Loyalty is defined as being faithful, being true to vows or obligations, or having an allegiance to someone or something. Not long ago we received a call from one of our long-term customers. Barbara called to tell us she was quitting our service. She had been with us for three years. Because of this the alarm bells went off and after several people had attempted to get her to stay, I called.

"Barbara, tell me what's going on. I thought we were sending you tons of great sales candidates. I looked at the application numbers and they are solid."

"Yes, we are real satisfied with candidates you are sending to us," she replied.

"So why are you quitting? We are doing a good job for you, right?"

"We've been real satisfied, but we just want to try something else. To see what else is out there."

Dogs are loyal. Customers—not so much. This is why the customer loyalty movement is built on a foundation of manipulation and tricks. Take the airline loyalty programs. Are these programs really about creating loyalty or plying you with perks and traps that make it hard to make a switch? I'm not saying this doesn't work. I've definitely spent money on tickets designed to protect my platinum status. But was I really loyal? I want you to consider one more thing: if businesses really believe that customers would show faithfulness, honor commitments and vows, pledge and show their undying allegiance, and honor their obligations, then why are there contracts? Why are lawyers employed to enforce those contracts? Why are there manipulative loyalty programs?

Why did Barbara leave my company to "see what else was out there?" To her, we looked the same as everyone else. There are almost 40,000 competitors in the online recruiting market segment. Yes, we delivered on our promise and she was satisfied with our results. What we failed to do was differentiate ourselves in a way that created an emotional connection with Barbara. After more research, I discovered that the account manager responsible for Barbara's account had not contacted her in three months. He wrongly assumed that just because we were delivering good candidates and Barbara was not complaining, she was satisfied and loyal. She left us because she didn't feel appreciated and respected. We neglected her emotions.

A focus on customer satisfaction and loyalty will no longer give you the competitive edge. In a hypercompetitive, global marketplace where virtually every product or service is the same when compared with competitors in the eyes of your customer, customer satisfaction is worthless and loyalty to your company is fleeting at best. Yes, that is what I said—everything looks the same—and I know that you have heard the words come out of your customer's mouth or said them yourself: "Look, these products are all the same; just give me your best price."

Perhaps, you say *no*! My product, service, or company is different. Let me tell you our features and benefits. Then you pitch: blah, blah, blah, blah. Well guess what? "I'm the customer and your competitor was just in here telling me the same thing and he said that *he* was different. So it still all looks the same to me."

Perhaps you truly do have a unique product or service. The question is, how long will that last until someone matches what you have or convinces your customer that they have done so?

In the twenty-first century, competitive advantages derived from, unique products are short-lived because competitors are able to quickly and easily duplicate or match your offering. Because everything (products and services) is perceived to be the same to today's savvy buyers, delivering an extraordinary customer experience has emerged as the single most important competitive advantage for B2B companies across all industries. This is why real competitive advantage in the business-to-business marketplace is created through human relationships. Account managers, sales professionals, and customer service professionals—the people who are most connected to customers—are on the frontlines of customer experience. They build unique and enduring emotional connections with customers. This is where the rubber meets the road in business to business if you want to create long-term revenue and profit streams.

Unlike virtually every book that deals with customer experience or account management, this book is not page after page of *what your company should do to change*. It is not a business strategy tome designed for boardrooms or stuffy executive meetings. Not that it should be ignored by upper management, because as leaders you must focus on aligning business resources to make it easier for frontline account managers to serve and engage customers on the emotional level.

Instead, this book is designed for account management and customer service professionals, primarily in business-to-business roles and secondarily for those with high-end B2C relationship management responsibilities. For those new to account management, my goal is to provide you with a firm foundation on which to build deep, enduring relationships with your customers. For veterans, it is to remind you why you chose a career in account management and customer service and provide you with actionable techniques for reconnecting with your customers and delivering a legendary customer experience.

What's Love Got to Do with It

Love is an intense emotion—a feeling of warmth, trust, and affection. When you are in love with another person, you always want to be together, and when you're not, you're thinking about being together because without them you feel incomplete. Love is a visceral connection.

"I love this guy!" Pete reached over and wrapped his arm around Jesse. Todd Miller, president of Isaiah Industries, had just given Pete a Dealer of the Year Award. Jesse was Pete's account manager. Over the course of the Isaiah Industries' annual dealer appreciation banquet, the word *love* was used by virtually every dealer to describe their relationship with Todd and his staff of account managers. It was impressive.

Isaiah Industries manufactures metal roofing tiles. It sells its products through a network of high-end roofing companies. I'd met Todd through my friend Dennis Deuce, who'd referred me as a keynote speaker at the annual dealer conference. As I observed the interaction between the dealer principles and Todd and his team, I knew that Isaiah Industries was special. Even back at the hotel, in informal conversations, the dealers spoke in glowing terms about their account managers and Todd. What I thought was significant was that the conversations were about the relationships they had built with their account managers: "Always there for me." "Takes care of any issue fast." "So easy to deal with." "Jumps in and helps with problems." "Never takes me for granted." "I love Janet." "We love Bill."

I called Todd after the conference and told him about my observation. I explained that my experience with dealer and channel conferences was that the dealers spend much of time complaining about the supplier company. His response was emphatic: "We put our dealers and our dealers' customers first in everything we do. Without our dealers, we don't have a business. We work to make their experience with Isaiah Industries personal and unique. We want that experience to be legendary throughout our industry. This is why each of our account managers takes a hands-on approach and builds personal relationships with our dealers. We want it to be easy and fun to do business with us and we never want any dealer to feel like we are not there for them or that we take them for granted. We love our dealers and we want them to love us back."

Love is not a term that is often associated with business relationships. Yet, I heard the word *love* used to describe how customers felt about their account managers and customer service reps many times over during my research for this book. Over and over again, buyers told me how much they *loved* their account managers. At one company that granted me permission to observe and interview their inside sales group, the team leader's first words on my arrival were, "Before we get started I want you to meet our best account manager, Kimberly. Our customers *love* her!"

My interviews with account managers, corporate executives, and buyers revealed an important commonality. The best account managers, the ones who built and maintained long-term relationships, grew their account base, and earned the enduring respect of their customers, were successful at creating deep emotional connections with their customers. Connections that were so visceral the only word that buyers and others could find to describe them was *love*.

Love. That was it. The real secret to delivering legendary customer experiences for B2B customers was through emotional attachment: deep visceral connections like Todd and his account managers had developed with their dealers. I observed that the very best account managers and customer service professionals had leveraged human relationship techniques to influence the behavior of their customers. They had learned how to make customers love them.

A Paradigm Shift—From Information to Empathy

Technology and communication have forever altered the speed of business. Companies have used technology to wring more productivity out of fewer people, and modern communication, though it has made it easier to reach anyone at any time, has actually pushed us further apart. The irony is that even as huge investments have been made in technology, communication, and systems for the express purpose of giving account managers more time with customers, there has been less focus on the interpersonal skills that are so important in human relationships.

A big part of my mission with this book series—*People Buy You*, *People Follow You*, and *People Love You*—is teaching the next generation of business people how to leverage relationship skills. I believe at the granular day-to-day level, account management and, for that matter, all business is just one person solving another person's problems. Those one-on-one interactions are the basis for customer experience and getting customers to love you.

In the twenty-first century, interpersonal relationships are more important than at any other time in our history. The real irony of our incredible advances in technology and the emergence of the social web is that it has removed barriers that for so long made communication slow, cumbersome, and expensive. At the same time, however, new barriers have been erected that inhibit interpersonal interaction. Technology has removed the need to actually speak to other people or even meet with others face to face. These changes in the way we communicate have made it necessary for business professionals to learn and adopt new skills for building relationships, and they have placed more value on traditional relationship-building strategies.

From the moment we entered the Information Age in the 1980s, process has been valued over people. The Internet and its accompanying technology wrung productivity out of every business process and system. As productivity per worker increased, so did our prosperity. As barriers to communication improved, we were then able to move the repetitive tasks that could be systematized overseas, where low wages helped boost profits even more. In less than two decades, we removed human interaction from many of our day-to-day activities. Just consider how online banking and stock trading have changed the way we interact with our financial institutions. Along the way, customer service deteriorated as many shortsighted companies shifted service functions overseas. You only need to reach a customer-service representative in another country who reads preapproved copy, like a robot, from her computer screen instead of actually showing empathy and helping you to know what I mean. Thankfully, many of these same companies, realizing that these interactions create negative customer experiences, are reversing those decisions.

This is why your role as an account management or customer service professional has become so important and critical. In the B2B environment, for many companies, the loss of even a single customer can create layoffs, close plants, and potentially threaten the future of the company. Account managers are very often the glue that holds these relationships together.

As an account manager or customer service professional, *protecting your company's customer base, the lifeblood of your business, must become your priority.* If you are not in there with your customers as a trusted resource giving them reasons to continue buying your company's products or services, then you are playing Russian Roulette with your revenue, bonus, and career.

In his bestselling book, *A Brand New Mind*, Daniel Pink makes the case that workers who have the ability to be empathetic and interact with others will have the competitive and economic edge in the coming decades. Pink makes us aware of the value of human interaction to our own success in both business and life. It is this understanding of human behavior, empathy, and the ability to leverage interpersonal skills that make people love you that will be your competitive edge and what makes you truly special and valuable in the experience economy

The objective of this book is simple. I want you to understand how important your ability to get others to like you, trust you, buy you, and *love* you is to your future and the future of your company. I will teach you how helping your customers get what they want (solving their problems) will reward you with what you want. While I will focus on how to influence human behavior, I will not indulge in long diatribes on human psychology and personality traits, or lessons on understanding the intricacies of body language and facial expressions. I won't be quoting from textbooks about the studies of famous scientists. I will not provide tricks for manipulating customers.

People Love You is a practical guide. It exists in the real world. My goal is to teach you techniques for interacting with customers in a way that creates deep, enduring relationships. I want your customers to love you. However, to create a legendary customer experience you must learn how to step into your customers' shoes and to feel and see things from their point of view.

Before moving on to the next chapter, take a moment to answer these questions honestly: "What is it really like to be *my* customer? How does it *feel*?"

2

The Seven Essential Principles of Customer Engagement

Let's get this straight from the get-go. You do not work for a perfect company or boss. Your product or service is flawed. Your support team, service delivery team, warehouse, billing department, help desk, technicians, engineers, installers, and so forth will make mistakes, show up late, and say stupid things to your customers. You will always have more customers and more on your plate than you think you can manage. Your customer will almost always want more than you and your company can or will deliver. Sometimes these demands will be unreasonable. Customers will almost always notice imperfections, call about service deficiencies, make demands, and inform you that your competitor is offering a huge price discount at the worst possible time.

This is reality. It is the reality that the vast majority of books and training programs on customer service and relationships brush over or ignore. It is why so many training programs fail to actually improve the customer experience. Salespeople, account managers and customer service professionals are left wondering if the trainer or author has ever actually managed a customer relationship. Most of these programs treat customer relationships as if they exist in the vacuum of a perfect world rather than being woven into the fabric of an imperfect and flawed business environment.

There is nothing easy about serving customers. Your job is hard, demanding and at times maddening because your role is to mitigate this imperfection and shape, mold, and influence the customer experience through human relationships. Of course if everything was perfect—customers never made demands and competitors never came calling—your company wouldn't need you.

I'll never forget my first call from Jeffrey. It was the Tuesday before Thanksgiving and I was on the road with my family on vacation. Two weeks earlier I'd been hired as a national account manager. I was taking over a portfolio of 30 strategic accounts, many of which had been ignored by my predecessor. When I answered the phone, "This is Jeb Blount. May I help you?" what followed was a string of expletives from a very unhappy customer. What was he angry about? No one had paid any attention to him. He was being taken for granted. There were service problems at his locations. The product we were delivering was damaged and lacked quality. Pick a problem and Jeffrey had it. He brought my competitor up several times and how they wanted his business. I just listened and let him rant. When he had gotten everything off of his chest, I agreed that he had received very poor treatment and asked him if he would give me a chance. I told him that the buck stopped with me and promised to fix the problems.

A week later we sat down at a coffee shop outside of Dallas and just talked. I went back the following week, visited his offices, and we had lunch. Jeffrey wasn't yelling any more. I made sure to deliver on any promises I made. We talked often and met in person when it made sense. Along the way we became friends. Over the next two years, Jeffrey's spending with me and my company increased from $500,000 to more than $5 million. He became one of my largest and most important accounts.

My company stayed the same, our product and service delivery did not change, Jeffrey's demands did not change, and my competitors worked their tails off to take his business from me. Yet, when his contract was up for renewal, Jeffrey signed an unheard of 10-year agreement (the average contract length in our industry was 3 years). Why? He trusted me. He believed that I was his *advocate* within my company and that I looked out for his best interests because I'd focused my time and effort on understanding his business, and personal motivations, and solving his problems. Years later, we are still friends and Jeffrey has made dozens of referrals that have allowed me to expand my business.

Seven Essential Principles of Customer Engagement

Customer service is most certainly given mere lip service in some organizations while others make massive investments in delivering truly legendary customer experiences. The same holds true for individual customer service and account management professionals. Some are extraordinary relationship builders while others consistently fail at the most basic element of the customer experience—human interaction.

Each interaction, no matter how insignificant, with a customer creates an experience that they feel and remember. These experiences are cumulative and over time become the foundation of long-term relationships and the glue that holds them together. Intuitively, you know that the relationships you build with your customers are more important than product, services, and price. You already have customers who *buy you* and *love you* because your relationships with them are so strong. Still, the human side of working with customers is a mystery to most people in business today.

People don't love companies, they love *you* and you don't serve companies; you serve *people*. Emotional people with their own agendas. Sometimes complaining, belligerent people who seem to lack any semblance of logic or reason. People who will almost always default to their own self-interest despite what you want or need.

Serving customers and delivering legendary customer experiences is at its core an emotional endeavor. It is personal for you and your customer. To think otherwise is to deny who we are as people. Human relationships are often illogical. They are guided by subliminal instinct and irrational emotions. Relationships with other people are complex and there are simply too many variables to get it right all of the time. Anyone who has dealt with customers will easily find stories and situations where they allowed their human, emotional side to cloud a relationship. As with all things, humans are fallible. We make mistakes. We are never perfect.

Yet there are certain foundational principles that will guide you through the process of working with customers. Principles are basic truths, morals, and ethical standards. As people we are inherently guided by our principles. Principles dictate our behaviors, decisions, and every aspect of our interactions with those around us. For this reason, the most successful account managers rely on a firm set of principles and values that guide them in customer relationships much as tracks guide a train.

My goal with this chapter is to ground you in a core set of principles that when internalized will help you engage customers and develop enduring relationships.

Principle 1: You Need Your Customers More Than They Need You

In business one principle stands above all: You need your customers more than they need you. If you only internalize one lesson from this book, make this the one. A basic understanding that you need your customers more than they need you is the single most important business lesson you will ever learn. Until you get this, and I mean really make this principle part of your heart and soul, it will be impossible for you to deliver legendary customer experiences.

Consider this: The number one reason companies fail is a lack of customers. What would happen to you if suddenly you had no customers? You know the answer and so do I. Your business would be in shambles and you would be unemployed. So who is more important—you or your customers? Your customers don't need you. You need them. Without them you have no job, you cannot feed your family, you cannot invest in your future.

Ineffective account managers and customer service professionals believe that they are more important than their customers. They think that they are indispensable to their customers. That customers are things or objects to be exploited, rather than people who should be served. They believe arrogantly that they are smarter and more competent than their *stupid* customers, and it shows in their actions and behaviors.

When you get your next paycheck, take a close look at it. The money that was deposited in your bank account was put there by your customers. Sure, your company's name may be on the check stub, but that money came directly from your customers because those customers chose to do business with you. You were rewarded because they spent money with your company. If you receive a bonus, or incentive, when customers pull back spending or go to competitors, it affects your paycheck. If you participate in profit sharing or own company stock, losing customers harms your future. If enough customers leave, it will eventually cost you your job. Therefore, anything you do that impacts customer relationships impacts you, your paycheck, and your family.

This is why top account managers put their customers first. They are driven to deliver the very best customer service. They are customer-centric. They enjoy serving their customers, and constantly seek ways to solve their customers' problems and bring new ideas to the table. Top customer service professionals believe their mission is to help their customers win and reach their goals. They are advocates for their customers. And they believe that by helping their customers reach their goals, they will reach their own.

Principle 2: Customers Are People

Customers are people. They are emotional, irrational, and human. They feel fear and stress. They are overworked and underpaid. They are time starved. They have ambition and goals. They have an insatiable need to feel important and appreciated. They have families and priorities.

Each interaction with a person creates an experience that they remember. Though you may believe that your product or service has a greater impact on your customer's experience than you do,

I assure you that this is not the case. Customers don't do business with companies; they do business with people—*you*.

When dealing with people, empathy is king. In other words, learning to step into your customers' shoes and see things from their human perspective helps you experience them as people. The Golden Rule—treat others in the same manner you want to be treated—is perhaps the most powerful and universal principle guiding human relationships. It is simple, straightforward, and far too often ignored. I've heard countless customer service reps complain about the poor customer service they receive and then go on to treat their own customers in the same manner or worse. The Golden Rule of customer relationships states that you should treat your customers in the same manner that you want to be treated. If you will just follow this core principle, you will find it much easier to view and treat customers as people.

Principle 3: You Are Always On Stage

Business is a grand stage and as a customer service and account management professional, from that stage you deliver customer experiences. Everything you say or don't say, do or don't do; your facial expressions, tone of voice, and body language can and *will* have an impact on your customer's experience. Your words and actions have meaning. A misspoken word, display of raw emotion, or slip of the tongue will impact the relationships you have with customers.

Imagine standing on a stage in an auditorium. In the audience are your clients. Your every behavior is being analyzed. You are being observed to see if your actions are congruent with your words. Judgments are being made about your dependability and how much to trust you. In account management and customer service, you are always on stage. You must exert a tremendous amount of self-discipline to manage every behavior, promise, and action while in front of your audience. This is where emotion collides with logic. This is where customer experience is born.

Principle 4: Customers Act on Emotion and Justify with Logic

One of the core principles at the foundation of the *People Love You* philosophy is a universal law of human behavior: *People act first (or buy) on emotion and then justify those actions with logic.* Every day as we go through life, we make hundreds of decisions. Some are big and some are small. Some are made based on pure intuition and others are considered until we feel good about our choice. Some people make decisions fast, and some people are slow to decide. Some weigh all of their choices while others jump right in. Regardless, emotions guide them in advance of logic. No matter what empirical evidence they have before them, action is driven first by emotion. This does not mean that facts, numbers, observations, and statistics are not important. Evidence and supporting data are critical in decision making. But it is the emotion we feel that causes us to act.

Now, there are folks who will argue this point to the death. Unwilling to admit just how emotional we are as humans, they point to themselves as examples. They offer eloquent rebuttals to explain that their decisions are made on facts and logic. In reality, though, after a little questioning, I am always able to point out that they have simply gone back and justified their initial emotional decision with logic. Hindsight is 20/20. We all do it. Business organizations realize that even the best purchasing managers, who are trained to buy based on facts and figures, are still swayed by emotion. In recent years, a few purchasing departments have even begun holding online, reverse auctions. The aim? To take the human element—the emotions—out of the purchasing process.

Principle 5: Customers Do Things for Their Reasons—Not Yours

Have you ever been baffled by a customer's decision? Ever had a customer quit you even though you were delivering a great ROI? Ever given a customer a proposal that would save him a ton of money and then watched him go in the opposite direction? It is frustrating and at times, mind numbing. Because customers are people, they choose to do things for their reasons—not yours.

No matter how much you plead your case or implore the person to do the right thing, unless she believes that it is in her best interest to do that thing, she probably won't. The most effective account managers take time to connect emotionally with their customers. They embrace the belief that though customers may not always be right, they are always first. They stand in their shoes and view situations through their customer's perspective. In this way, they are able to shape customer decisions because they better understand their customers' motivations, fears, desires, needs, and wants.

Principle 6: Customers Don't Do Illogical Things on Purpose

When I teach this principle in seminars and trainings, invariably someone will say, "Looks like you haven't met my customers." You may be thinking the same thing because, like me, you've observed customers do some really dumb things. What is important to understand, however, is no one wakes up in the morning, looks into the bathroom mirror, and says "You know, today I think I'm going to sabotage my vendor or my business by doing something really stupid." No, for the most part (with perhaps a few isolated situations), customers don't do illogical things on purpose. There usually is an alternative explanation for their actions.

Mediocre account managers believe that customers do dumb things on purpose. They shake their heads, throw their hands up, and blame their customers. These same managers, when customers call with problems, focus on proving their customer wrong rather than understanding why there is a problem. Often these account managers are condescending, short, and rude to their customers because they believe the customer is stupid.

Top customer service professionals assume *positive intent*. In other words, they recognize that the customer thought she was doing the right thing. They know that when a customer is doing the wrong thing, there is a reason and it is in their best interest as a service provider (because they need their customers more than their customers need them) to investigate *why* the person is doing something that seems illogical rather than simply judge it as such. This helps them to either gain understanding or uncover and remove the root cause.

Principle 7: Always Give More Than Is Required

Any conversation about serving customers compels me to address what is perhaps the most overused string of useless words in the pantheon of customer service clichés: *exceeding customer expectations*. If you are serious about delivering legendary customer experiences, please do yourself a favor and wipe this inane phrase from your jargon vocabulary. It might sound great on a marketing slick and provide a feel good moment in a company meeting, but it is a delusional mindset at best and an ineffective way to manage your customers' overall experience.

Think back for a moment on the opening story in this book about my flight to Chicago. Following the flight on which my experience was so bad, I quit flying the airline. Question One: Was I satisfied? Answer: Yes. The airline got me to Chicago in one piece for a low price. Question Two: Did they exceed my expectations? Answer: I expected to take off late, get there late, and potentially lose my bag along the way. I realize this sounds like a low expectation, but if you travel a lot you tend to lower your expectations. In this case, they got me there a little early and my bag was waiting. So yes, they exceeded my expectations. Question Three: Did my experience stink? Answer: A resounding *yes*!

At my company, we have a simple value statement that we live by. *We always do more than we have to and we will be kind to everyone, no matter what.* Why don't we use the same tired old, *We exceed customer expectations*? Because it is not possible to do and, as I just illustrated, exceeding expectations does not necessarily create a better experience.

The fact is customer expectations are both individual and fluid. In some cases, those expectations can be tangible like a project deadline or getting a passenger to a destination on time. In most cases, though, it is hard to know and impossible to control what your customer expects and even if they tell you what they expect up front, that expectation is likely to change over time.

So instead, focus on what you can control—your actions. Your customer pays you for a product, service, or plane ride. Your choices in that exchange are to give them (1) less value than they paid for, (2) exactly the value they paid for, or (3) more value than they paid for. You have complete control over that choice. When you give more, your effort does not go unnoticed because it is in our nature as humans to recognize people who go the extra mile for us. It makes the experience of spending our money or doing business with someone more pleasurable. We forget about our *expectations* and instead focus on how good we feel.

Recently, one of our account managers here at Sales Gravy was working with a vice president of sales for a major engine manufacturer. Our customer needed to recruit a salesperson with a specialized background and had come to us after firing several other firms who were unable to deliver. The problem for us was the search was so hard that we were not sure we could deliver, either. A month into the search, we had gotten nowhere. Concerned that we would be next on the chopping block, I checked in and was surprised to find that our customer was very pleased with our effort. He said, "It is frustrating that we still don't have a hire, but your guy is working his tail off for us. I get daily updates on candidates and I can tell he is taking this personally."

Imagine that. We were not coming even close to meeting our customer's expectations. Yet, he was thrilled with the experience of dealing with a professional who was giving far more than he had to in a nearly impossible situation. Furthermore, because our customer saw how hard we were working, he trusted us when we told him that we were turning over every stone. Instead of firing us, like all of the firms before, he extended our agreement and placed his bet on the person he could see was going the extra mile and giving more than he had to give.

3

The Five Levers of Customer Experience

Serving customers is hard and, in many cases, thankless work. As an account manager or customer service professional, you are placed in a position to solve customer problems and fix issues caused by flaws in your company's product or service that are beyond your control. You are often tasked with cleaning up the mess left by the salesperson who closed the account while that same salesperson is getting pats on the back or even bigger rewards for the sale. You receive little glory for your efforts. No one seems to notice when your customers are happy and your accounts stable, but when customers are upset or defect to competitors, you are the first one to catch hell.

As account managers and customer service professionals, you must deal with emotional, and often irrational, customers on a daily basis—customers who *demand* attention. You are called upon to deal with irate customers who yell, scream, and threaten. If this isn't hard enough, you must protect your accounts from competitive encroachment; renew contracts; negotiate rates; and deal with policy wonks, Peter Principle executives, clueless engineers, and bureaucrats who have no idea what it is like to serve customers on the front line.

Today's account managers are placed under unyielding pressure to perform. In the twenty-first-century business environment, there is little patience for account managers who lose customers and fail to grow their business base. It is no longer about what you have done; it is about what you have done *today*.

It is a wonder why any sane human being would voluntarily choose to serve customers. Yet, millions of people serve customers as account managers and customer service pros. Unfortunately many are ill prepared to perform the job and become the fodder of countless stories detailing the hapless mistreatment of customers. The good news is that some of these people will become well-loved, superstar account managers. They will build enduring, unbreakable relationships with their accounts. These men and women are not one hit wonders. They consistently do this year after year, delivering legendary customers experiences.

Why do some people make such great account managers, while so many others fail miserably? We set out to uncover the answer to this question. We interviewed account managers, customer service professionals, buyers, CEOs, and other corporate executives from a wide cross-section of industries. We pondered our own experience both as customers and serving customers. Through this process, we discovered that account managers who are loved by their customers and have the uncanny ability to deliver legendary customer experiences demonstrated five core behavior patterns.

In rare cases did these behaviors come naturally. The people we interviewed told us how they learned these behaviors from mentors, training, watching others, and mostly through trial and error while learning on the job. These revelations support our firm belief that customer relationship skills can be taught through accelerated learning. Certainly one must have some innate talent and social skills for dealing with people. However, proficiency with the process for working with and building relationships with customers are learned behaviors.

I call these behaviors levers. I use the term *lever* because a lever is a simple tool that has the potential to produce tremendous force and move large objects. The Greek physicist and mathematician, Archimedes, said, "Give me a lever long enough and a fulcrum on which to place it, and I shall move the world." Likewise, the *Five Levers of Customer Experience* work together in helping you move people to love you by tapping into the motivations that are driven by human emotion.

Five Levers of Customer Experience

How do you keep your customers happy? How do you keep your customers from defecting to competitors? How do you get them to buy more every year? What is the secret to getting customers to love you? How do you deliver a great experience?

Consistently effective customer service is such an elusive mystery that quite literally thousands of books and articles have been written on the subject. Customer service fundamentals are taught in universities, corporate training programs, and stand-alone seminars. Every business has customers and the ones who want stay in business seek out resources (books, articles, training programs, seminars) that help them better serve their customers. Most of these resources are excellent and worthwhile. Yet, most focus on the mechanics of customer service and account management rather than the underlying emotional elements inherent in human relationships.

I did not set out to write a dissertation on the mechanics of customer service. Instead, my intent is to focus your attention on the most fundamental, and important, aspect of customer experience in business-to-business account management—*developing, nurturing, and leveraging the interpersonal relationship between customers and account managers.* Mechanics are useless in the absence of strong relationships.

The fact is customers love *you.* Not products or services. Not low prices. Not your company. Not slogans or cool branding. It is your ability to get your customers to believe in *you* and trust *you* that plays the most powerful role in delivering legendary experiences.

You start by *putting your customers first.* Putting your customer first means placing their needs and goals before your own. This opens the door to building an emotional *connection* because your customer believes you have their best interests at heart. The more connected your customer feels to you, the more comfortable they feel sharing information that reveals their problems and issues. With this information in hand, you can focus on and solve their real problems. *Problem solving* is at the heart of customer experience and customers are extremely loyal to people who solve their problems. Customer relationships, however, are built on a foundation of trust. Because of this, you must take careful steps to *build trust* through your actions, demonstrating that you are dependable and do what you say you will do. Finally, you reinforce and anchor their emotional connection and trust in you with *positive emotional experiences.*

Put Customers First

Putting customers first is an attitude. It is a deep, internalized belief that the customer is more important than anything else in business. Customers first is a belief system that helps you override your natural tendency to focus on what is easy and pleasurable for you and instead step into your customers' shoes to see things from their perspective and change your behavior to serve their needs over yours—to make it easy and pleasurable to do business with you.

Connect

Like all interpersonal relationships, connections bind customers and account managers together on an emotional level. An intense focus on building sincere emotional connections with customers is critical to delivering a great customer experience. Connecting tears down walls that tend to get in the way of real communication and understanding. When customers feel connected with you, they feel more comfortable telling you their real problems, roadblocks, and issues. With this information in hand, you have the opportunity to solve problems that really matter. This provides real value for your customers and engenders true loyalty. Most important, when your customers feel connected to you, they will be willing to accept your advice, feedback, and suggestions, which is critical to problem solving. Strong connections are hard to break and are the foundation of truly prosperous, enduring relationships built on mutual trust.

Solve Problems

When you strip everything else away, customer service and account management is about one thing: One person (You) helping another person (Your Customer) solve a problem. Problem solvers are the champions of the business world. A solved problem is at the heart of the customer experience. It is what customers pay for. Solving problems is the foundation of the *People Love You* philosophy. The fact is, people are extremely loyal and become emotionally attached to people who solve their problems. Solving problems is about helping your customers get what they want. When you help your customers get what they want, you will get what you want. You will grow your customer base, gain praise from your boss or company, earn a higher salary, qualify for incentive bonuses, and ultimately feel good about *you*.

Build Trust

When customers rely on you to deliver on promises, they are putting themselves in a vulnerable position with their money, time, and in some cases, their jobs. Your customer's reliance on you creates such vulnerability that, should you fail to perform, the impact on their business, company, or career could be extreme. Trust is the sole foundation on which the relationships you build with your customers rest. Every action, decision, and behavior links to and directly affects trust—positively or negatively. Without trust, your customer's experience is one of uncomfortable suspicion, anxiety, anger, and ill will. Without trust, there will be no repeat business. You will not retain or grow your accounts. Without trust, your reputation suffers. No matter how good your product or service. No matter how well known your company brand. No matter how likable you are, how hard you work, how many problems you solve, or how many nice things you do, you absolutely, positively cannot deliver a legendary customer experience without trust.

Create Positive Emotional Experiences

Creating positive emotional experiences for customers allows you to take advantage of the Law of Reciprocity, which states that when you give something of value to others, they will feel obligated to give something to you in return. When you consistently create joy in the lives of your customers you build emotional bonds or anchors. Just as an anchor is used to hold a ship in place against currents, wind, tide, and storm, positive emotional experiences do the same for relationships. Positive emotional experiences help you build enduring and unbreakable relationships with your customers.

Account management is hard work. It requires loads of self-discipline and sacrifice. From time to time, you'll have your heart broken and your ego injured. There will be disappointment, mistakes, and failure. Sometimes you will fail—not because of ill intentions but because you are human and not perfect. Serving customers can also be incredibly rewarding. You have the opportunity to build and nurture long-term relationships and to be appreciated for your efforts. As a problem solver, you have the opportunity to make a real impact on your customer's organizations. This is an amazing feeling.

The Seven Essential Principles of Customer Engagement will guide you as you grow as an account manager. The Five Levers of Customer Experience are foundational behaviors that keep your relationships grounded and on track. In the following chapters, you will learn that when you make these levers an integral part of your life as a customer service or an account management professional, you will consistently deliver legendary customer experiences, and *people will love you.*

4

Put Customers First

"I'm sorry, we can't get started until we have all of the proper paperwork completed."

Chris paused outside of Janie's office and listened in. He'd been on his way to a meeting but on overhearing her conversation with one of their clients, stopped in his tracks.

"Yes sir, I understand that you are under a tight schedule, but it all has to be filled out correctly." Her voice was stiff and admonishing.

Chris could hear a man yelling on the other end of the line from all the way out in the hall. Then Janie raised her voice.

"Look Dan, you can call Aspen if you want to but you signed a contract and in that contract it says that you are responsible for getting us the proper paperwork on time and complete." The man was yelling again.

"No, I can't do it for you! I realize you're busy. I'm busy, too. You're just going to have to find a way to get it done. The regulations won't allow us to go to work until the proper paperwork is filed."

Chris heard the phone slam down and stuck his head in the door. "Hey Janie, sorry, but I couldn't help overhearing your conversation, what was that all about?"

Janie looked up, startled to see her CEO standing in the doorway. "It was Dan Edwards from over at the Radner site. He is insisting that we have our trucks over there tomorrow. I've explained to him a dozen times that we can't get started without the proper paperwork!" Chris could hear the frustration in her voice.

"Well, what's missing?" He asked.

"It's the same thing with all of these customers! He didn't fill in the environmental form completely. We can't send it to the EPA that way or they will send it back." She reached behind her and grabbed a thick stack of papers off her credenza and shook it at Chris. "You see this? We've got almost 30 jobs on hold because these customers (her tone was biting as she emphasized *customers*) can't get the required paperwork in right the first time!"

"Let me see that." Chris reached across her desk and grabbed the stack of papers from Janie's hands. He did the math in his head as he thumbed through the incomplete forms. There was almost $15 million in revenue just sitting there waiting on paperwork. He'd been on his way to a meeting with his executive team to discuss strategies for getting revenue up. The company was behind on its numbers and the Board was looking for answers. Fifteen million dollars and Janie was just one of his project managers. *How many more jobs were held up because of paperwork,* he wondered, *and how many customers are we pissing off in conversations like the one he'd just overheard?*

"Janie, how much is Dan's job worth?"

"I don't know. I think about $600,000," she answered.

"So for $600k, couldn't we just finish the paperwork for him? Wouldn't it make more sense to get the job started and the revenue in than to hassle the guy about incomplete paperwork?"

Janie shifted in her chair. When she spoke, it was clear that she was on the defensive. "That's not my job. That's the customer's job. As soon as we start doing paperwork for them, they'll just dump it all on us and unless you are going to give me an assistant I don't have enough time for that."

Chris could tell he wasn't going to get anywhere with Janie at the moment, so he thanked her for helping him understand and continued on to his meeting. He'd been brought in three months earlier to turn the company around and had already observed several opportunities to improve customer experience. "But this was an in-your-face moment of clarity," he explained. "That conversation told me that our people did not understand who paid the bills. We had millions of dollars in revenue sitting on our project managers' desks because helping customers with paperwork *wasn't their job.*"

The next afternoon, Chris gathered the project managers and executive team in the conference room. When everyone was seated, he asked, "Why don't jobs start on time?"

"Incomplete environmental paperwork," several people replied. Others nodded in agreement.

"What do customers hate the most?" he asked.

"Filling out paperwork," more people replied.

"What causes the most dissatisfaction and conflict with customers?"

"When we don't start their jobs on schedule," replied Denny, the vice president of operations.

"And why don't we start their jobs on time?" asked Chris.

This time, everyone around the table replied in unison, "Paperwork."

"Folks," Chris looked toward the project managers and continued, "I've polled each of you and we've uncovered $27 million in projects that we could start today if we just had the paperwork ready. The vast majority of those stalled projects are waiting on paperwork we kicked back to our customers. If we get those projects started now, it will go a long way toward helping us dig ourselves out of our financial hole. That is why you are here; I want your ideas on what we can do."

Janie sat back in her chair, arms crossed, and answered, "I know you want us to say we should do the paperwork for them. Like I said before, as soon as we start they'll just dump all of their paperwork on us and we don't have time for that." The other project managers nodded in agreement.

Chris turned to Tom, the company's CFO, and asked, "Tom, what happens if we don't get the revenue from these projects?"

Tom looked down at the spreadsheet before him on the conference table. "If we don't get this revenue booked, we are going to miss our number in a big way. A miss that big is going to cause us to come close to breaking our bank covenants and that's really going to have the board of directors breathing down our necks."

"What does that mean, Tom—in plain English? I'm not sure everyone here understands the consequences of breaking bank covenants." Chris gestured toward the project managers.

"Bottom line?" Tom asked bluntly.

"Bottom line." Chris responded.

"It would be very bad. It means that we would have to cut expenses to the bone, and start laying people off. If we miss badly enough, we might even have to file for bankruptcy to reorganize our debt. If that happened, many of us could lose our jobs, as well."

The room fell silent as the gravity of the situation started to sink in. Chris got to the point. "The one thing that pisses our customers off the most is when we don't start jobs on time. The reason that happens is they hate doing paperwork. This causes conflict between you and our customers and that leads to a poor customer experience. What we need as a company, more than anything right now, is revenue. That revenue is in our hands and all we need to do is get the paperwork completed. If the paperwork is complete, we can start the jobs. That makes our customers happy and reduces conflict. Happy customers tend to give us more business. Janie, I'm having a hard time seeing this from your perspective."

Janie softened her voice. "But Chris, there is still information that only the customer can provide."

"Okay, I understand that. But how much of the form could we complete without the customer's input?"

Terry, another project manager jumped in. "Honestly, most of it. There are only a handful of fields that only the customer can fill in."

"Good, Terry," Chris smiled. "How do you think the customer would respond if we sent them the forms with almost all of the fields completed?

"I think they would be shocked." Sara, the vice president of sales, chimed in. "They hate our paperwork. If we showed up with most of it already done it would be so much easier on them. They would love it and we could sell that."

Then Janie added, "If we are going to go that far already why not just go the rest of the way? We could call the customer and get their specific information and then just send them the completed form for signature. That would really blow their minds."

Chris smiled. "Great idea, Janie! Just think how much better the entire experience would be for everyone and how much more business we could gain from happier customers. What we have to understand is we cannot survive as a company without customers. If we don't put our customers first, they will go to our competitors. I'm not saying that it will be easy to change the way we do paperwork and we are going to have to juggle some other things to make that happen. From what you are saying, though, it will make it easier and more pleasurable to do business with us."

Chris and his team got to work and reprioritized. Six months later, things were much better. They had reduced contract to project start time by 95 percent and customers were raving about the service they were getting from the project managers. "And revenue was up, way up," Chris explained. "It is hard to believe that something so small can make such a large impact. But I think it is important that we never forget to spend time standing in the customer's shoes. That is how we learn what it takes to put them first in everything we do."

Bridging the Experience Gap

During my interview with Chris, we discussed the *Experience Gap*. This is the gap between what your customer really wants and what you want. The good news is, essentially, you and your customers effectively want the same thing: You both want the experience of dealing with each other to be easy and pleasurable. The problem is that what *easy and pleasurable* means to you is not necessarily what easy and pleasurable means to your customer. To deliver a great customer experience, you must first bridge this *gap*.

Let's take a look at this concept based on Chris' story:

	Janie	Customer
Easy	Customer sends in completed paperwork on time and I don't have to chase them down for it.	No complicated paperwork. No hassle getting my project started.
Pleasurable	Customers rarely call and when they do they are not demanding. They just call to tell me how happy they are.	When I call, my project manager is helpful, kind, and attentive to my needs.

The Experience Gap is normal—it's human. As people we naturally default to our own selfish wants and needs. Of course, we would prefer if all our customers were pleasant to deal with. It would be so much easier if they never had problems or complaints; were self-sufficient; never demanding; and only called to say how happy they are with our product or service. Let's be honest. If you've been servicing customers long enough, on occasion, you've indulged in the thought: *this would be a great job if it wasn't for all of these customers.*

This is why *Customers First* is more than a slogan. It is a belief system and attitude that helps you override your natural tendency to focus on what is easy and pleasurable for you and instead become empathectic to your customer's point of view. A Customers First attitude helps you adjust your behavior to better serve your customer's needs over your own.

Putting customers first is an attitude—a deep, internalized belief. It is something that happens on the inside first and then manifests itself in your daily actions and behaviors. Unfortunately, I can only teach you what this belief looks like and the techniques for developing it. I cannot create a customer first attitude for you.

It is a choice you make and something you will need to develop on your own.

The most effective way to develop this belief system is by cultivating *empathy*. In other words, try to see and feel things from the other person's perspective. That's easy to do because you are somebody's customer, too. You spend money and you have had great experiences and terrible experiences. You already know how it feels so consider these questions:

- What do my customers want to experience?
- Is it easy for my customers to do business with me?
- Is it pleasurable for my customers to do business with me?
- What changes do I need to make to deliver a better experience for my customers?

Your customer's experience is complex. It is shaped by the things you control like your actions and behaviors and things you cannot control, such as your company's products, services, and delivery systems. Your customer also brings their own beliefs, attitudes, and past experiences to the mix. As frustrating as it may be, you can only impact your customer's experience through the things that are under your control. Though you may believe that things beyond your control have a greater impact on your customer's experience than you do, I assure you that this is not the case. Customers don't do business with companies, products, or services; they do business with y*ou*.

Make It Easy for People to Do Business with *You*

Companies like Amazon and FedEx dominate because they have made it so super easy to do business with them. When companies make it hard for customers to do business with them, those customers will eventually go somewhere else. As a consumer yourself, you can surely remember a situation when you've had a hard time doing business with a company and made the choice to go somewhere else with your money.

The most progressive, customer-centric companies and executives are fanatical about standing in their customers' shoes and removing any friction in the customer experience. Far more companies, especially those serving other businesses, have either on purpose or inadvertently raised barriers that make doing business with them difficult and frustrating for customers. (If you are an executive with the ability to influence change, find these barriers and start removing them.)

As a customer service or account management professional, it is likely that you have little influence over the barriers your company has raised that make it hard on your customers. Instead, you are tasked with mitigating these obstacles and helping your customers get around them. I know this can, at times, be frustrating and even maddening, but it comes with the territory. The objective of this book is not to discuss how you can change your company; it is to help *you* become the competitive differentiator with customers. Instead of focusing on what is wrong with your company, tackle the one thing you can control—You.

Is it easy to do business with *you*?

1. Do your customers have all of your contact information? Do they know the best way to reach you when they have an urgent need?
2. Are you accessible? Do you answer your phone, text messages, and e-mail when customers call?
3. Do you quickly follow up on voice mail, e-mail, and other messages? Or do you ignore or put off customers you know are going to complain?
4. Do you provide regular, proactive updates on projects, deliveries, reports, or other outstanding deliverables?
5. Do you do what you say you are going to do? Do you meet deadlines? If you can't keep a promise or deadline, do you call your customer in advance and let them know?

6. Do you show up on time to appointments, meetings, and calls? When you must be late, do you call in advance and let your customer know?

7. Do you quickly deal with complaints and follow up to ensure your customer is happy with the resolution?

8. Do you check reports, invoices, letters, and presentations for accuracy, typos, and consistency before they are sent to your customers?

9. Do you maintain copious notes from meetings and conversations with your customers and log them into your CRM?

10. Do you proactively offer solutions to your customers' problems? Do you schedule regular, formal account review meetings with your customers?

11. When customers have problems, do you respond quickly and provide regular updates until the issue is resolved?

12. Do you call your customers on a systematic basis to check on them and offer help or do you wait for them to call you?

13. Do customers have to chase you down and nag you about promises and deliverables?

14. When customers call you for help with a problem, do you act like (or make them feel like) it is a hassle? Do you give them a hassle?

15. Are you a pleasure to do business with?

While you consider these questions it is important to make an effort to see the answers through your customers' eyes. You may even want to ask them what they think. Never forget that your customer's experience begins and ends with how easy it is to do business with *you*.

Likability Is the Gateway to Connections

The word *likable* is defined by the Merriam–Webster Dictionary Online as, "having qualities that bring about a favorable regard." Being likable is not a guarantee that your customer will *love* you.

As you will learn, it takes far more than likeability to deliver a legendary customer experience. However, if you are not likable, your customer will not enjoy doing business with you. It will not be a pleasurable experience.

If you are unlikable, your customers will eventually leave you for a competitor who is more pleasant to do business with. In our seminars and corporate training programs, I always ask to see a show of hands from those who like spending time with unlikable people. I've never had a hand go up. The fact is, you do not enjoy being around people who are unlikable, and you avoid these people whenever possible. Your customers are no different. If you are not likable, you have virtually no chance to build a lasting relationship.

Likability is the gateway to emotional connections and long-term customer relationships. When customers find you likable, their natural emotional walls come down and the door opens to a profitable business relationship. Likability is sort of like *relationship glue*. Likability impacts how customers perceive you, as well as their willingness to engage in conversations and allow you to solve their problems. In addition, it affects their desire to give you second chances when inevitable mistakes and service issues occur. Without it, you simply cannot and will not connect with customers.

The cliché "You never get a second chance to make a first impression" is an obvious play on words designed to illustrate the importance of first impressions. We all make instant judgments when we first meet people. Those judgments, which are both imperfect and emotional, have a lasting impact on how we view and interact with others. These same judgments are being made by your customers about you.

How long does it take for others to judge you as either likable or unlikable? An instant! Unlike trust, which is earned over time through many interactions, being perceived as likable or unlikable occurs in mere moments. So, when first meeting new customers and contacts, it is critical that you control the behaviors that impact likability.

Some people are naturally likable. When they show up, the room lights up. They have appeal to a wide range of people. Others naturally gravitate to them and they make friends easily. These rare and gifted people, more often than not, have no idea why they are so likable. They have God-given talent and operate from pure instinct. They are naturally pleasant, have friendly facial expressions, and are talkative but not arrogant. We all, to some extent, have characteristics that make us naturally likable to others. We find it easy to connect with and develop relationships with certain types of people and personalities. People tend to be attracted to people who are like them.

The problem we face in business, though, is that we don't always get to choose the customers we interact with. This means that many of the people we encounter will not be attracted to us naturally. Complicating things are the preconceived perceptions that all people bring into relationships. These perceptions may include cultural, racial, socio-economic, and behavior style biases that are beyond your control.

There are, however, behaviors that are in your control that make you more likable. These behaviors neutralize biases and open the door to connections and relationships with a wide range of people. Unless you have a natural God-given talent for being likable, you will have to work at and consciously practice these behaviors. Prior to meetings and interactions with customers, you will need to remind yourself to practice likable behaviors. For example: If you are naturally more of an introvert, then you may have the tendency to feel insecure around strangers. This insecurity translates into behaviors like avoiding eye contact or displaying body language that suggests you lack confidence. To be more likable, you will have to overcome your natural instincts and, instead, make eye contact, pick your shoulders up, and smile confidently. The same goes for many natural behaviors that impede likability. You must develop the self-discipline to remain consciously aware of your behaviors and be prepared to adjust those behaviors to the people with whom and environments in which you find yourself.

Is this easy? Well, no. If it were, we would all seem more likable to one another. Changing natural behaviors is never easy, no matter what the endeavor. The vast majority of people in the world walk through life allowing their natural behaviors to negatively impact their current and potential relationships. These individuals are unwilling to make changes. Unfortunately, they are naively unaware of the impact this has on their success.

Likable Behaviors

Clearly, there are many things that influence likability. However, as I said, there are fundamental behaviors that universally impact likability, and these attributes are completely within your control. Flexing your style, smiling, good manners, being there, enthusiasm, confidence, and authenticity are behaviors that make you seem more likable to others.

Flex Your Style

Flexing your style essentially means adjusting your approach and interpersonal behaviors for each individual so that they are more comfortable working with you. We each have a unique style of dealing with the world around us. Some people are direct, while others beat around the bush. Some people talk slow with little emotion, while others are more animated. People may be ambitious and driven, analytical and careful, or social and outgoing. My intention is not to educate you on different personality styles but to reinforce that when you flex your style to your customer, it improves communication and your relationship. Becoming a master at flexing your style requires knowledge of your own preferred style, keen observation, and the discipline to self-correct.

When you are aware of your personality style and how you respond to specific situations and to other styles, it gives you a powerful competitive advantage.

The best way to understand your behavioral style is to take a personality assessment (or several). There are literally hundreds of assessment tools that will provide you with a picture of who you are. Some of the more popular assessment tools include Myers-Briggs, DISC, Clifton Strength Finder, Kolbe, and my own Personal Style Inventory.

As an account manager, it is your responsibility to adjust to your customers. You need them more than they need you, so if your style impedes your relationship, you are hurting your own success. The good news is that small adjustments in your style often make a big impact. Once you are aware of your style and the preferred styles of your customers—with conscious effort, and a little flexibility—you will find that getting in sync with them will make you more likable.

People Respond in Kind

Take a look around you. Notice how few people are smiling? Now try this experiment. When they look up at you, smile at them. I've found that nine out of ten times they will smile right back. When that happens—you smiling at them and they smiling at you— for just a moment, you have an instant connection.

When it comes to likable behaviors, people tend to respond in kind. This is why these behaviors are so effective at neutralizing personality, cultural, and style biases. Savvy customer service and account management professionals use this to their advantage with angry and upset customers. No matter how rude or angry the customer is, they remain calm, respectful, and pleasant. The customer calms down, and in many cases, will apologize for their behavior.

People respond in kind. When you are polite, they tend to be polite. When you are respectful, it is likely you will receive respect in return. Enthusiasm can be transferred. And when you smile, most people will smile back at you. Because people respond in kind, you have the opportunity to control the tone of most of your interactions with customers. Instead of being at the mercy of circumstances, you can influence the emotions customers feel by simply managing your own behaviors. When your actions make your prospects and customers feel good, it influences the quality of their experience doing business with you.

Smile

Have you ever interacted with a customer service representative who never smiled? Remember how it made you feel? There is a saying: "Frown and you frown alone, but smile and the whole world smiles with you." From the moment of birth, we learn that smiling is the fastest way to get others to pay attention to us. A baby's smile lights up the room. Smiles attract. Frowns repel. Even dogs understand this. A wagging tail, upturned mouth, and bright, wide eyes are the fastest route to a pat on the head or treat.

Numerous scientific and psychological studies have shown that the smile is a universal language that is recognized across cultures and ethnicities around the globe. Studies have also shown that smiling is social—we smile far more with other people than we do when we are alone. Smiling is a primary communication tool used to connect with and bind us to others. The smile has the ability to convey meaning depending on its intensity. Excitement, humor, pleasure, confidence, happiness, openness, love, understanding, caring, kindness, and friendship are all communicated through the smile.

Though there are volumes of research on the importance of the smile in human behavior and communication, we don't need a researcher to explain the obvious. The smile is the most effective way to instantly connect with another person. We are attracted to people who are smiling. We yearn to join groups of smiling people because their smiles tell us they are happy, and we want to be happy. Smiles also set people at ease and create a relaxed environment. Your sincere smile says, "I mean no harm. I'm open." In this relaxed environment, you will find that people are more likely to talk to you, more willing to answer your questions, and more open to connecting and developing a relationship.

When you are smiling, you discover that people are more willing to help you. People will offer you a hand and go the extra mile for you. When you are smiling, people are more forgiving of mistakes and more understanding of your faults. A sincere smile humanizes the relationship between you and your customer and conveys authenticity. Victor Borge once said, "The shortest distance between two people is a smile." There is simply no substitute for the smile when it comes to making it pleasurable for customers to do business with you.

Why Don't People Smile?

Take a walk through your company's offices, the mall, down the street, in public places, and look around. You will notice many dour, serious faces. Consider the many encounters you have with customer service reps who don't smile in person or project the image of a smile through their voices over the phone. Why, if smiling is such an important part of human communication and critical to delivering a great customer experience, are so few people smiling? The simple answer is they are thinking about something else—usually themselves.

In social situations, smiling comes naturally in response to others. It is innate, instinctual, and automatic. When someone says something funny or greets you with a smile, you smile back.

But when you are not prompted to smile by the people around you, especially when dealing with upset customers who are not smiling, it is natural to forget to put a smile on your face or in your voice.

When people are not smiling, it is most often not because they are unhappy, but rather because they are lost in thought. Unfortunately, when you are lost in your own thoughts, you are not that likable. This is not such a problem for a mailroom clerk or a bookkeeper, but it is a big deal for account managers and customer service representatives who depend on relationships with others.

When you walk into appointments with a client or pick up the phone to make a call, what do they see or hear? How do customers perceive you? Do they see a smiling, upbeat, and likable business professional or a serious, self-absorbed, unapproachable person? You control these perceptions, and perceptions have a tremendous impact on your likability.

Because smiling is not a natural state outside of social situations, you must consciously make the effort to put a smile on your face when meeting others or when picking up the phone. The key words here are *conscious* and *effort*. Making a conscious effort means.

- Being aware of where you are and those around you.
- Pushing your own thoughts aside.
- Putting a smile on your face even if initially you have to fake it.

Smiling in social situations is easy; doing it in the real world so that it appears spontaneous and sincere takes practice. A technique some people use to smile naturally and sincerely is to just think of something pleasant. This has the added benefit of lifting your mood. It is easier to smile when you feel good and are thinking about happy things. Thinking about something pleasant also helps you relax and improves your confidence—two keys to smiling naturally. I like to look in the mirror before I walk in to see a customer (or get on the phone) and practice smiling. If I'm in the parking lot of my next appointment, I'll look in the rearview mirror and smile—big and wide. It looks ridiculous but by the time I walk into the building I'm greeting everyone from the security guard, to the receptionist, to my client with a pleasant, friendly smile. And because people respond in kind, it doesn't take long for the people I meet to smile back at me.

Take a moment and consider the last time someone you do business with greeted you with a big smile. Chances are it made you feel great. You knew they were glad to see you and it made you happy to see them. That is one of the best things about a smile. Dale Carnegie put it best: "When you greet people with a smile, you'll have a good time meeting them and they'll have a good time meeting you."

Be Authentic

In business situations, it is often tempting to pretend to be someone or something you are not. When you feel this temptation, it is your ego speaking. It is a desire to rise above your lack of self-confidence by being misleading or phony. Insecurity and lack of self-confidence are at the heart of inauthenticity. Negative self-talk and the subconscious belief that you are not good enough tempt you to say or do things that compensate for these feelings. Most people are gifted with the intuition to see right through this. They know when things do not seem to add up or if you seem fake. Once they do, your trustworthiness and integrity are immediately in question, which diminishes your ability to build connections and trust. Think about it. When people are not authentic with you, how do you feel?

Authenticity is the child of confidence. When you develop and maintain self-confidence, you overcome the temptation to pretend to be something you are not, in order to stroke your own ego. You have enough trust in yourself to keep it real and be yourself. In terms of likability, being yourself equals being human, which is far more likable than any fake personality you conjure up.

Of course, dealing with customers requires a high level of professionalism. With customers, being yourself does not mean acting the way you would with a bunch of your college buddies. Manners, respect, and etiquette remain important. You must balance being a real human being with interpersonal skills that allow you to be empathetic, open, sensitive, diplomatic, and real.

Be Polite and Respectful

When I was a kid and we would go places, my mother would sit us all down and sternly remind us to *mind our manners*. My brothers and sisters and I were not perfect, but over the years, with my mother's constant reminders (she still reminds of our manners today), we learned etiquette and how to behave properly around others. Likewise, at some point in your life, you were taught basic manners and etiquette. Although you may not know which fork to use first at a formal dinner, you know right from wrong, the difference between being rude and polite, and how to be respectful of others. Almost everyone, at some point in their lives, has been exposed to good manners. Yet, as illustrated time and again in stories about bad customer experiences, many people choose—yes, choose—to be self-centered and to focus only on themselves and their own needs.

Have you noticed how many mean, nasty, ill-mannered, rude, and disrespectful people there are in the world today? It seems as though rude people are everywhere. Rudeness and impolite behavior have become so prevalent that in many cases it is just accepted as normal. I once saw a bumper sticker that read MEAN PEOPLE SUCK. They do! No one really wants to be around people who are rude and lack manners. No customer says of her account manager, "Did you see how rude John was? What a jerk! I hope he comes by again soon, so we can spend more time together." Rude, impolite people are not likable. As a customer service professional, failure to adhere to basic manners and rules of etiquette will damage your relationships and make dealing with you an un-pleasurable experience.

Good manners will not only help you deliver a better customer experience; they'll help you advance your career. With so many rude people working in customer service, there is a real opportunity to stand out and make a great impression solely on your behavior. These days, good manners seem so rare that when you are consistently kind and polite to those around you, people notice and remember you. Good manners are appreciated and give you a competitive edge.

Fortunately, using good manners and etiquette is completely within your control. All you need is a little self-discipline to focus on those around you rather than on yourself. Use the Golden Rule as your guide. Just treat others the way you would like to be treated. This means everyone from the janitor to the CEO. Being polite only to people who matter to you in a business sense demonstrates lack of character and is disingenuous. Besides, you never know who is watching.

Respect and manners go hand in hand. Rude conduct generally shows a lack of respect, while well-mannered behavior is indicative of respect. I grew up in the South, where we were taught that it is proper to address those older than you or in a position of authority with *yes, sir* and *no, sir* and *yes, ma'am* and *no, ma'am*. While I realize that this is a regional and cultural characteristic of the American South, because this practice so clearly demonstrates respect, it has served me well all over the world.

You may show respect in many ways. Shaking hands and making eye contact demonstrates respect. Listening to others, being appreciative for help that is given, and waiting for others to be served before eating at business meals are all ways to show respect.

When you give respect, you will get respect from your customers in return.

Failing to focus on the person you are interacting with is patently disrespectful. If you've ever been in a conversation with another person who looks away, distracted by something or someone else, or interrupts you to return a text message or e-mail, you know how disrespected this makes you feel. When you don't feel that the other person is listening to you, it hurts your feelings, makes you feel unimportant, and in some cases, just makes you plain mad. When you are interacting with a customer, *be there*. Turn everything else off, remain completely focused, and do not let anything distract you.

In today's demanding work environment, it is easy to become distracted. The ubiquity of smart phones, tablets, and mobile computing has consigned us to constantly looking at our devices. Cell phone calls interrupt conversations. E-mail and the Internet distract us while we are on the phone and in meetings. The late Jim Rohn said, "Wherever you are, be there." This is essential advice when it comes to demonstrating respect in interpersonal relationships. To deliver a great customer experience, you must develop the self-discipline to shut everything else out and remain completely focused on your customer.

Finally demonstrate respect for your customers by using "please" and "thank you." When you show your gratitude, it will not go unnoticed. It is a true sign of respect when you take the time to just say *thank you*. It demonstrates that you are not taking your customer for granted. There are few gestures more impactful than a simple thank you.

Be Kind

At my company, Sales Gravy, our value statement reads, *We will be kind to everyone, no matter what*. Many customer service professionals and account managers have gained the reputation of being short and rude to customers. Being overly demanding, demonstrating impatience, and generally showing a lack of kindness all conspire to damage your likability and credibility, and ruin your customer's experience. You should never forget that someone you have been less than kind to may be just the person you will need help from in the future. When dealing with customers, practice being cheerful, polite, calm, respectful, and appreciative, no matter how they treat you. Treat them the way you wish to be treated. More often than not, people will respond in kind. Take our motto as your own. Be kind to everyone, no matter what. I guarantee that your reputation as a professional will grow in the wake of your kindness.

Compliment Often

Abraham Lincoln said, "Everyone likes a compliment." I once worked for a man who had a habit of complimenting everyone he met. He was an executive running a 2-billion-dollar-a-year business—the big boss. He traveled the country visiting his company's offices and production facilities. Wherever Steve went, the people at his plants looked forward to his visits. Everyone from the part-time worker picking up trash in the parking lot to the top managers received a sincere compliment whenever he was around. They would kill for this man. Anything he asked for would be done. Not because they had to do it, but because they wanted to do it.

One of the easiest ways to be likable and win others over is to offer a sincere compliment. Developing awareness of others will help you notice things about them to compliment. The key is to put your own self-centered thoughts aside and become genuinely interested in other people. When you give customers a genuine, sincere compliment about a trait, possession, or accomplishment, you've given them a valuable gift. You make them feel valued, acknowledged, and important. Most important, when people feel this way, their self-esteem goes up, they like themselves more, and because of this, they find you likable.

When I smile and others respond in kind, I like to compliment them with, "You have a great smile." Each time I do this, their grin gets even bigger. Compliment clothes, handsome kids, awards, children's artwork, or personal traits. If you know the person well or have done research in advance of meeting them, compliment an achievement. The key is training yourself to be interested and observant of others. When you do, you will be amazed at how far a sincere compliment takes you.

Passion, Enthusiasm, and Confidence

Passion, enthusiasm, and confidence go hand in hand, because they are external manifestations of inward beliefs, feelings, and attitudes. Passion for serving customers and enthusiasm for projects, goals, products, and services draws customers to you like a magnet. Confidence in yourself and your talents is essential to authenticity, solving problems, and having the courage to challenge customers to make changes that are in their best interests. Passion and enthusiasm in the right measure is infectious. Confidence in the right measure provides your customer with a sense of security that you have their back.

Time out for a moment of truth. When your alarm goes off in the morning, do you wake up ready to serve your customers and take on new problems, or do you dread going into the office and working with all of those idiot customers you've had the misfortune to have assigned to you? Do you feel a sense of self-worth when you help a customer or do you feel as though your customers are draining every ounce of energy and joy from your life?

If the latter sounds like you, *stop now* and take a close and honest look at yourself in the mirror. Be truthful. If you are not happy dealing with customers, you will never create legendary customer experiences and they will never love you. You'll just be another bad experience customers complain about. Go do something that makes you happy. Life is too short to do something you hate and at the same time make life miserable for the customers who are counting on you.

Passion is intense enthusiasm for something. For account managers and customer service professionals, that *something* must always start and end with *helping customers solve problems*. Working with customers is hard work that many times comes with little reward. Customers will let you down. They'll quit after you have invested your heart and soul to save their account. They'll be rude. It is easy to become cynical. Passionate account managers, however, see past these setbacks and focus instead on the incredible feeling they get from building relationships with people. Passion moves customers because they can see how much you care. Passion is a far more influential motivator than logic or facts.

Because passion is emotion, it cannot be taught or learned; you either have a passion for dealing with customers or you don't. You cannot fake it. A true unbridled passion for solving customer problems gives you resilience in the face of failure, persistence when confronted with roadblocks, and the strength to be true to the principles, values, and convictions that are so important for delivering legendary customer experiences.

Be Enthusiastic

Enthusiasm is simply having excitement for or interest in what you are doing. What we have already learned about human nature is that people respond in kind. If you are enthusiastic about something, it is likely that those around you will become enthusiastic, too. The good news is we generally find enthusiastic people likable, and we are more likely to accept their point of view. This is why enthusiasm is such an important tool for account managers.

The question that always arises when discussing enthusiasm is, "How do I become enthusiastic about a product, service, idea, or company that does not excite me?" First, you have to realize that the vast majority of people in business do not work in glamorous industries or with glamorous products. Of course, some people work for companies like Apple where it is easy to get enthusiastic about the cool products. But most of us work for companies in which the products and services are mundane. The key here is to find something to become enthusiastic about. I've got a good friend who manages industrial uniform accounts. He's been doing it for 31 years. He loves it. His enthusiasm is effusive. It is not the uniforms that get him excited, though. He loves working with his customer base. He is enthusiastic about finding solutions to his customers' diverse set of problems.

One of the fastest ways to become enthusiastic is to learn to appreciate the things about your company, product, service, or career that excite you. Train yourself to look for and find the positives in every situation and focus on those things. If there is absolutely nothing about your situation that you can be enthusiastic about, I suggest you find something else to do quickly. Customers, managers, and peers can tell when you lack enthusiasm. As Vince Lombardi famously said, "If you are not fired with enthusiasm, you will be fired with enthusiasm."

It is likely, though, that your situation is not so dire and all you need to do is prime the enthusiasm pump. That means you might have to fake it until you make it by demonstrating the enthusiastic attitude that you would like to create. In other words, you might have to pretend for a while by playing the part. Dale Carnegie taught that when you act enthusiastic, you become enthusiastic. It works this way because when you act in a certain way long enough, subconsciously those actions eventually define who and what you become.

Be Confident and Courageous

One of the most important keys when working with customers is your confidence and courage to be decisive. Think about it: Do you enjoy being around people who lack confidence? Neither do your customers. And customers hate dealing with account managers who are afraid to tell them the truth.

Self-confidence is a balance. On one end of the spectrum, there are those who lack any confidence. These *weak* people are unlikable and ineffective at dealing with customers. On the other end of the spectrum, there is overconfidence. Arrogant people, though sometimes successful in the short term, eventually crash and burn, undermined by their false conviction that they are superior to those around them.

Confidence is driven by your self-image, self-esteem, attitude, experience, knowledge, and skills. Your confidence naturally goes up or down, depending on specific situations. However, confident people have an underlying belief in themselves that transcends situational issues; it is this self-confidence that empowers them to be adaptable to the unpredictable environment around them and to deal with uncertainty.

This core confidence stems from a belief that no matter what happens, they will find a way to succeed. Perhaps the best description of this underlying belief is Henry Ford's often quoted line, "Whether you think you can or you think you can't, you are right." Your aptitude for developing confidence plays a critical role in your career. Not only do your customers feed off of and draw strength from your confidence, it also gives you the courage to make decisions *in the moment*, when you don't have all of the information, to confront customers with the truth, and to stand up for your company and convictions.

Unfortunately, as you well know, confidence is a complicated emotion involving many internal and external influences. Regardless, you can learn to develop and maintain confidence; it will just take time, experience, and persistence. You have the power inside you right now to develop confidence, even if you don't feel particularly confident at this moment. The process of improving or building your confidence is as simple as your choices. You choose what to believe about yourself and your abilities. You choose how you will approach your customers. You choose to improve your knowledge and do your homework. You choose to invest in yourself—mind, body, and spirit.

What do you believe about yourself and your ability to succeed? What are you afraid of? It is easy to find out. Just listen to your self-talk. Above all things, your self-talk has more impact on your confidence than anything else. You talk to yourself constantly. This ongoing internal conversation will either lift you up, giving you courage and confidence, or pull you down. Fear, uncertainty, and doubt are the reason for most negative self-talk. World War I Ace Eddie Rickenbacker was quoted as saying, "Courage is doing something you fear." He also said that courage cannot exist without fear. Rickenbacker believed that fear was natural and that it was overcoming fear that created courage. He believed that it was okay to feel afraid, but it was just not okay to allow fear to hold you back. The people who develop courage and learn to be courageous, over time, reap the most success and rewards. Just ask this honest question of yourself: *What would you do if you were not afraid?* Fear is holding you back from something in your life.

Developing courage rather than running away from fear helps you improve your confidence. Rickenbacker had it right. Fear is a requirement for courage. When you learn to use fear to systematically practice and build a strong foundation of courage, over time your self-confidence becomes unwavering. The secret is using fear, the way a bodybuilder uses iron to create muscle mass, to exercise and build your confidence.

When a bodybuilder first starts working out, he uses light weights. Slowly, day after day, repetition after repetition, he adds weights, until soon he is lifting two, three, or four times as much as when he started. In this same way, you can build a strong foundation of courage and confidence. Just take small steps. There is certainly no way to overcome all of your fears. However, when you make it your mission to overcome one or two things you fear each day, you'll make real progress.

Keep track of your accomplishments to build your self-confidence. Soon, a little bit each day, your confidence will grow stronger.

Invest in Yourself

Maintaining a confident and enthusiastic demeanor is difficult in the brutal business environment of the twenty-first century. Technology and communication have increased the speed of business and leveled the playing field among competitors. The pace of business in today's environment is faster than at any time in the human experience. The pressure and demand to perform is unrelenting. You must deliver results or else. Today, companies demand more productivity, shorter sales cycles, and higher margins, from fewer resources. You can be the hero one day and the goat the next.

The demands of the modern workplace conspire to eat away at your confidence, enthusiasm, and passion. The mental and physical toll on today's customer relationship management professionals is brutal. As the advocate for your customers, you battle for them daily. You remove roadblocks, deal with your company's bureaucracy, and solve problems. You deal with back orders, delivery issues, and billing mistakes. You answer to the boss. You fight the office. You fight for contract approvals, for credit approvals, and resources to serve your customers. Every problem, every roadblock affects your attitude and diminishes your enthusiasm. At the end of the day, you go home. You deal with your spouse, your kids, your pets, your neighbors, the bills, and a million other things. Your energy is drained, your belief system deteriorates, and the stress takes a physical toll.

When you are tired and burned out, you are not a pleasure to do business with. You lose your self-discipline to put customers first, you make poor decisions, and you lack the energy to invest in relationships. Customers are counting on you, so to combat this

fatigue you must take steps to invest in yourself: *mind, body, and spirit.*
You have to take time to re-energize and build your confidence.

Invest in Your Mind

Gandhi said, "We should live as if we will die tomorrow and learn
as if we will live forever." Account Managers who continually
invest in their knowledge are happier, more motivated, confident,
effective, and invariably more likable. The most successful business
professionals have a passion for learning. They take advantage of
every training program their company offers and are always the
first people standing in line when there is an opportunity to learn
something new. They attend and invest their own money in conferences, seminars, and workshops to keep their skills updated and
sharp. They read constantly and are rarely caught without a book.
They subscribe to podcasts, weekly e-zines, trade magazines, and
business publications to stay current on their industry. They understand that by investing in the mind, they acquire the knowledge and
skills required to outpace their competitors, thus becoming valuable
assets to their companies and most importantly their customers.

Invest in Your Body

Dealing with customers is a mental game. You use your mind to
solve complex customer problems rather than physical might.
However, thinking requires a tremendous amount of energy.
Your mental energy is limited by your physical energy, so becoming
physically fit naturally boosts mental energy. Major studies have
proven that regular exercise improves creative thinking, mental
clarity, and the capacity to bounce back from inevitable rejection.
Investing in your appearance is also an important step in building
your confidence. When you look good, you feel good. Customers
love winners, and winners look and feel confident.

Invest in Your Spirit

I've interviewed hundreds of successful people on the subject of spirituality. At the core, this group of highly successful people, all from different backgrounds, believe that there is something or someone bigger than themselves working in their lives. They believe that everything in life is connected, and they have faith that everything happens for a reason. They believe that a higher good is looking out for them and wants abundance in their lives. They believe that through service to others they gain true fulfillment. They also believe that the spirit requires nourishment, exercise, and constant attention.

Investing in your spirit is, in essence, an investment in a strong belief system. Your belief system is the foundation for your values, principles, attitude, and confidence. For instance, if, like the people I mentioned in the preceding paragraph, you believe that everything happens for a reason, your perspective and attitude on potentially negative events will be optimistic. Instead of complaining, "Why me?" you ask, "How can I learn from this?" Your beliefs have a direct impact on your confidence, passion, enthusiasm, likability, and ultimately, the quality of the experience you deliver to your customers.

Turning First Impressions into Lasting Impressions

It is important to note that likability can be fleeting. In new relationships, first impressions are turned into lasting impressions when your behavior remains consistent. A rude remark, an inconsiderate act, a slip in your confidence, or losing your temper can quickly turn positive first impressions into lasting negative impressions. In business relationships, you must never forget that you are always on stage and being observed by your customers. In an imperfect world with imperfect personalities and unpredictable circumstances, you must employ self-discipline and vigilance to ensure that you consistently manage the elements of likability that remain in your control.

Of course, the longer and more connected your relationship becomes, the more forgiveness and leeway you will be given. This does not mean you can take these relationships for granted. In business, that is the fastest way to lose. The same actions that helped you make a good first impression, repeated again and again, keep these relationships anchored and profitable. We'll explore anchoring in greater detail in Chapter 8.

5 | Connect

Roger was empathetic and calm as he gently nodded his head and looked up at Joanne. "Joanne, I understand, and you shouldn't have to feel this way," he said reassuringly.

Moments before, she had ripped him a new one. Joanne was the buyer for a large food processing company and Roger's company was a key supplier. The previous account manager had left the company several months before and, for reasons that no one could really explain, the account had been left unmanaged.

Joanne had invoicing issues, delivery problems, and quality deficiencies. She had made numerous attempts to reach her account manager (of course, no response because she was no longer with the company). She had also made four calls to customer service—all unreturned. She was frustrated, feeling that the company no longer cared about her. Under pressure from her plant manager, whose production line was being negatively impacted by these issues, she had started the process of finding a new vendor. She also sent a scathing letter to Roger's corporate office letting them know in unequivocal terms that she would be terminating their contract.

That letter set off a panic across the organization. The account was large and profitable and losing it to a competitor would not only be a financial setback to the company but also provide red meat for competitors who would use the loss to lure other customers away. The vice president of Roger's region assigned him to save the account.

Roger protested. "Look, Tim, you guys are sending me into a no-win situation. From the looks of things, there is no saving this account. I don't want to end up being the scapegoat here because someone else screwed up. I'm a company guy and willing to do my part, but this is unfair."

"I hear you," Tim responded. "But I need you on this. They are one of the largest customers in the region and we cannot afford to lose them. Our guys down there messed up royally on this one and I know it is not fair to ask you to stop what you are doing and clean up their mess but if anyone can turn this around, it's you. I'm counting on you to save it."

What could Roger say? He booked himself on the next flight out and prepared for the worst.

You Can't Make Me Love You If I Don't

Even as I write these words, I can hear Bonnie Raitt's voice wailing, "I can't make you love me if you don't." When I first broached the title of this book, *People Love You*, to one of my CEO friends, he shot back, "You can't make people love you!" He's right: You cannot make people, lovers, or customers fall in love with you. They must choose to love you, on their terms. If they choose not to love you, there is nothing you can say or do to change their minds. You simply cannot *talk* or argue a customer into loving you, your company, or your product.

It is like trying to argue someone into agreeing that they are wrong. You may eventually wear them down until they capitulate. Yet, as they walk away they'll still believe that they are right and you are wrong (or a jerk depending on how hard you argued). To catch a glimpse of this human behavior in action, spend an evening watching interviews on cable news shows. The host lobs a controversial subject to two experts with differing beliefs about an issue. Then they argue and shout each other down. Do any of these people ever change their opinions? Not on your life.

Though debate can be effective for developing and vetting ideas, it is only effective in situations and environments where there is a basic foundation of trust and consent by all parties to engage in debate to create better solutions. For example, if your customer invites you to a meeting for the express purpose of getting your ideas on how to improve a business situation and in that meeting you challenge an established process or practice, you have a chance to change their view because they view you as a trusted advisor and they want to change.

In the next two chapters, you will learn more about how to solve problems and build trust so you become a trusted advisor and resource for your customer. In this chapter, you will learn how to open that door by building strong emotional connections.

Like you, customers have strong emotional attachment to ideas, brands, companies, and people. When they have an emotional attachment to you, it makes life much easier because their emotional walls come down and they give you the opportunity to focus on and solve their real problems. When your customer feels connected to you, they treat you like a member of their team rather than a vendor that they keep at arm's length. Long term, they renew contracts and give you even more business. However, if you have not established a connection with your customer, you'll find yourself in cold conversations, bickering over price and contract terms, constantly fighting to keep the business you have, and eventually you will be locked out and replaced by a competitor.

You Cannot Argue Customers into Believing They Are Wrong

When Jennifer was in her sophomore year of college, she decided to join her school's student newspaper staff as an advertising salesperson. As a business major, she thought the experience would be a valuable addition to her budding resume. The paper paid a small commission for advertising sales that she hoped would provide some spending money.

On her first day, she met with the editor to discuss advertising accounts. During the meeting she asked about the Ford dealership that was near campus. The editor just shook his head and said, "Don't waste your time there. The owner of the dealership got mad at us a few years back and won't buy any more ads. He throws anyone we send over there out."

Jennifer defiantly marched right over to the dealership and asked for the owner. "I just let him talk. He told me the newspaper hadn't been responsive and didn't show his dealership the respect he thought it deserved. He vented and I listened. The longer he talked the less he vented and the more he talked about what he wanted. He eventually told me that he really wanted to advertise with the paper because the students were good customers for used cars."

"I responded, 'It isn't fair the way you've been treated by my newspaper. Your dealership is such an important account for our newspaper and you deserve to be treated that way.' Then I asked, 'What if I was your main contact and if you needed anything you could just call me?'"

"He started grinning and said, 'I like you.' He said he would buy more ads as long as he could just deal with me. Then we talked about an ad campaign and I took his order. When I got back to campus and showed the editor, his mouth dropped open."

Every account executive the paper had sent over to the dealership had tried to *talk* the owner into placing more ads. They believed that they could argue him into changing his feelings about the paper. Jennifer won him over because she was likable, listened to him, and made him feel important. As soon as an emotional connection was established, he gave her the opportunity to solve his problem.

Real Connections

Almost everyone has at least one person in their life with whom they have a real, lasting connection. These connected relationships are usually with spouses, best friends, or family. The deep emotional connections they share are characterized by descriptions like "this is someone I can talk to about anything." When you have problems in your life, this is the person you go to first for help because you know she will listen. Because she listens, you feel that you can reveal what is really happening—your real feelings and problems—instead of hiding them as you do with others.

Of course, these deep emotional connections are personal and different from business relationships. However, the principle is the same. In all relationships—business and personal—the more connected you feel to another person, the more you are willing to reveal your true feelings and problems.

The most important role of an account manager or customer service professional is helping customers reach their goals. The challenge in this is uncovering roadblocks, issues, and problems that you are in a position to remove or solve. Unless your customers feel some sort of connection with you, they will be reticent to tell you their *real problems*, to reveal their real emotions relative to those problems, and to accept your recommendations. Just as putting customers first is the gateway to connecting, connecting opens the door to problem solving, trust, and ultimately long, enduring relationships.

The Problem with Rapport

The Merriam-Webster Dictionary Online defines *rapport* as "relation marked by harmony, conformity, accord, or affinity." According to Wikipedia,

> **Rapport** is one of the most important features or characteristics of unconscious human interaction. It is a commonality of perspective: being "in sync" with, or being "on the same wavelength" as the person with whom you are talking. There are a number of techniques that are supposed to be beneficial in building rapport such as: matching your body language (i.e., posture, gesture, and so forth); maintaining eye contact; and matching breathing rhythm. Some of these techniques are explored in neuro-linguistic programming.

Rapport is a popular and ubiquitous concept applied to business relationships. A module on rapport is included in virtually every customer service and sales training course. You'll find a chapter or section on rapport in most customer service books. Hundreds of seminars are dedicated exclusively to the concept of rapport. A quick search on Google for *how to build rapport* yields more than 2 million results. Despite all of the books, seminars, articles, and corporate training programs, rapport is among the most misunderstood and misapplied concepts in business. Ask 10 people to explain rapport and you'll get 10 different answers. I know from experience because I ask the question of every group I train. The sad fact is few people have a clue what rapport is or how to *build it*.

Rapport is essentially being in sync with another person to the extent that you are able to influence their behavior. The rapport-building process is designed to develop common ground with another person through mirroring and matching body language, voice tone and speed, word patterns, eye movement, and even breathing. In time, according to the experts, when you truly have rapport with someone, you have the ability to lead them and change their behavior patterns. A process called neuro-linguistic programming (NLP), which embodies these techniques, including word-pattern matching, eye movement, facial expressions, and more, is espoused by many rapport experts as the real key to relationships and influence.

The problem with rapport is that it is just too hard and complex to get in sync with someone enough to influence behaviors. I'm not saying it is impossible for those willing to dedicate themselves to years of practice to become competent in NLP techniques. However, the reality is, despite promises from experts, these techniques are far too complicated for normal people. Few account management professionals have the time or inclination to become experts in deciphering word patterns, eye movements, and facial expressions.

Learning to effectively and discretely mirror and match people based on their communication style—audio, visual, or kinesthetic—sounds really cool in a seminar, but it rarely succeeds consistently in real world business situations with real customers.

This doesn't mean that finding common ground is a bad thing. The more you have in common with others—the more they are like you and you are like them—the easier it is for them to connect with you. If you find common ground, use it to your advantage to build emotional connections.

Take, for example, behavioral styles and personality types. We know that when people share the same behavioral style, they will naturally feel more connected. If you don't share the same style as you customer, you will develop a better connection when you flex your style to interact with them based on who they are—not who you are. The most effective account managers are masters at this. They are keenly self-aware of their behavioral style, values, and beliefs, and they are confident enough to adjust their style to deal with people who are not like them. The fact is, if your style makes your customer feel uncomfortable, developing an emotional connection will be more difficult.

The real problem with styles is that you are who you are, and that is not going to change; and your customer is who she is, and that is not going to change. Therefore, it is your responsibility to adjust to your customer. The good news is small adjustments in your style often make a big impact. However, even after you become aware of your own style and how it impacts others, it is unlikely that you'll get your customers to sit still long enough to take a style assessment and then discuss their style traits with you so you can adjust your communication style. For this reason, you'll need to use study and common sense to assess your customers' style preferences.

This is the dilemma in traditional rapport building. Because it requires so much awareness and focus, it often comes off as awkward, cheesy, manipulative, and insincere when applied incorrectly. Legions of business professionals who do not have behavioral style awareness fill in the gap with small talk about some random object in their customer's office, the weather, or a sporting event. Customers find these lame attempts at rapport building gratuitous and insincere. So much so that, over time, they become numb to rapport-building efforts.

The Real Secret to Connecting

There is a quote from Abraham Lincoln that aptly sums up why *building rapport* as a relationship strategy fails. Lincoln said, "If you would win a man to your cause, first convince him that you are his sincere friend."

Rapport is designed, not to develop trusting relationships, but rather to influence behavior. Rapport in its purest form is manipulative. Customers who feel manipulated will be distrustful of your motivations, no matter how pure, and will never feel connected to you. Connecting, on the other hand, is designed to win others over through a focus on them. The most effective strategy for winning others over and delivering legendary customer experiences is to start and end by helping them get what they want the most: to feel appreciated, valued, heard, and important.

Roger leaned forward and nodded slightly. "You shouldn't have to feel this way," he said to Joanne. He was relaxed, calm, and completely sincere. He is a master at making friends out of customers. Watching him work, I learned more about human behavior than in any book or training program.

For a moment there was just silence as Roger paused to let the words sink in. Joanne's body was tense, her face locked in an angry glare. "Joanne, I'm curious, were you part of the decision to choose us as your vendor three years ago?"

Joanne nodded. "Yes, I was responsible for looking at all the proposals and I made the final recommendation to pick your company." She relaxed just a little, yet her wall was still up.

"So, not only did we cause you a great inconvenience, we also made you look bad to the production manager," Roger shook his head in disgust. This was the breakthrough. He was on her side. You could see it in her face. Little by little, the tension lifted from the room. Roger had opened a crack in Joanne's cold, angry veneer. He'd demonstrated that he cared and was listening. He had empathy for her pain.

"Joanne, the way we have treated you is unacceptable and I want you to know how sorry I am for causing you to feel this way. I know you said that this meeting is a waste of time because you have no intention of giving us a second chance and I appreciate that you at least gave me the opportunity to apologize in person. I'm curious to know something, though. Why did you end up recommending us back then?"

Joanne told the story of how she had picked his company three years ago, and Roger just listened. By the time he left, Joanne was smiling and she and Roger were acting like best buddies. As he'd listened to her, the emotional wall between them crumbled and she'd talked herself into giving him a second chance. No matter what she said, he never tried to talk her out of a belief or argue her to his side. He simply asked questions and listened. To be sure, there was a long list of issues to address, yet there was a chance at redemption because Roger made Joanne feel appreciated and valued.

The most insatiable human desire and our deepest craving is to feel valued, appreciated, and important. The key to connecting and winning others over is, therefore, extremely simple: make them feel important. The real secret to making others feel important is something you have at your disposal right now. It's listening. Listening is simple and very powerful. When you listen, you need not worry about your communication style clashing with your customer's. When you shut up and give another person your sincere and complete attention, the ploys embedded in traditional rapport building techniques are made obsolete.

The ability to listen patiently is the skill that makes Roger so effective with customers. I've observed him with dozens of customers with diverse personalities and styles. Roger's behavior is always consistent. He asks questions and listens. His customers love him for it because instead of worrying about style points, he makes people feel important, valued, and appreciated.

The formula is simple: The more you listen, the more customers will love you. Unfortunately, no one is really listening. I realize this is a harsh and general indictment of virtually everyone, but it is true. We would rather think about and talk about ourselves, our wants and needs, our accomplishments, and our problems. If people aren't talking over each other in their eagerness to express their own self-important point of view, they are waiting impatiently for the other person to stop talking so they can start. The vast majority of people never make the effort to sincerely listen to others. Instead they talk at them. And when they are not talking, they're thinking about what they are going to say next.

It is not your fault that listening is not natural. To be self-absorbed is part of being human. You don't enjoy listening because listening doesn't make you feel important. Trust me, you are your own favorite person. The desire to feel important, valued, and appreciated is just as insatiable to you as it is for your customers. Yet, it is holding you back.

There is real power in understanding this basic tenet of human behavior and using it to your advantage. When you learn to overcome your self-centered tendencies and instead really *listen* to your customers, you will build strong emotional connections that truly differentiate you from your competitors. Although truly listening to another person requires self-discipline, selflessness, practice, and patience, it is not complicated or complex. That is the beauty of connecting. Unlike the complexity of rapport, connecting requires only that you listen.

The Fine Art of Listening

Have you ever noticed how often you have a conversation with your spouse, friends, children, boss, or customers, and shortly afterward, one or both of you disagree about what was said or agreed to? (This happens far too often with customers.) How is it possible? You were both there, either on the phone or staring at each other face-to-face, and you each walked away with a different understanding.

The state of listening in customer service is abysmal. Just reflect on your own experience when you have needed help, and you'll know I am right. Every training, every book, and every seminar on customer service has an admonition that listening is the key to success with customers. There is a reason. Listening is the most valuable skill for dealing with other people and yet the least practiced. Most people wonder (sometimes outloud), "Why doesn't anybody listen to me?"

Back when I was in fourth grade, my teacher, Ms. Gibbons, took the entire class outside on a warm spring day. She lined us all up, about 25 kids, and on one end of the line whispered a message, which she read from an index card, into the ear of the first child in line. That child then turned to the next person in line and whispered the same message. The process continued as each fourth grader whispered the message to the next in line until we reached the end. Ms. Gibbons then had the last child repeat the message out loud to all of the other children. There were giggles and snickers. We were all shaking our heads. The words that came out of the last child's mouth were not what we had passed on. Finally, Ms. Gibbons read from the index card. The words she spoke were foreign to almost everyone except the first few people in line. Over the course of 25 repetitions, the message had been so convoluted that it no longer resembled the original. The demonstration of how poorly we listened was so impactful, it has stuck with me my whole life. I think about it each time there is a breakdown in communication, which is actually a result of a breakdown in listening.

Despite all that we have been taught and all that we know, listening is still the weakest link in human interaction. Of course, it is likely that you already know this because you are interacting with people and they are not listening to you. It is likely that you have thrown your hands up in disgust and said, "Why won't these people listen to me?" or "What do I need to do to get my message through to them?" or "My [*kids, husband, wife, friends, employees, customers*] just don't hear what I'm saying!" It is frustrating, and it makes you feel unappreciated and unvalued.

If there is any good news, it is that you are not alone. It turns out that feeling this way is the human condition. It seems nobody is listening. Everyone is frustrated. We all want to be heard. As account managers, we scream out silently from the inside (and sometimes out loud), "If these customers would just listen to me, we wouldn't have any problems around here!"

Why does this happen and what can you do about it? The answer is as simple as it is complex. The reason people don't listen is that listening requires effort and focus whereas *not listening* is easy. It is hard to tune out all of the distracting noise; it is hard to be patient and wait your turn; it is hard not to look down at your phone, tablet, or computer screen; and it is very, very hard to turn off your own thoughts long enough to really pay attention to another person. Do you ever wonder why customers seem disengaged and don't listen to you? Well, when you are talking, it is easy for people to tune you out. But tuning out is a lot harder to do when you ask questions and get them to talk. When they are talking, they have to be engaged.

Unfortunately, it is so much easier for you to do the talking. When you are talking, you feel important, and you are able to get to the point faster and move on to the next pressing issue. You operate in a fast-moving and demanding environment. It is hard to take time away from all of the reports, gadgets, conference calls, and e-mails to listen to customers. This is especially true when a customer is trying to talk to you about something that is not an immediate priority. You blow her off or give her only part of your attention because what she is saying isn't important to you at the moment.

As an account manager, this behavior is hurting your relationships. One of the top complaints customers have about those who serve them is that they don't listen (in close relation to "they don't understand my business"). When your customers don't feel heard, they eventually shut down and stop bringing issues to you. This is how account managers get broadsided by a customer who leaves them for a competitor out of the blue. When asked independently why they went through the pain of switching customers rather than talking to their account managers about fixing the problem, the answer is often, "He wouldn't have listened to me anyway."

When you get into a regular habit of listening to your customers, they believe that you care about them. When they feel you care about them, they in turn care about you. This emotional connection builds trust, which is the critical foundation for relationships. So how do you learn to listen effectively?

- Read books about listening skills?
- Attend another seminar or training session?
- Hire a communication coach?

The answer is simple. Just pay attention to the other person. Amazing, isn't it? If you want to listen better, then give the other person your undivided attention. In other words—*be there*. Just become genuinely interested in the other person and hear what she is saying with all of your senses.

Sounds effortless, right? Well, not exactly. It is easy for me to say the words "give others your undivided attention," but in practice, it is very hard do. You, like most people, developed the habit of being self-absorbed over the course of a lifetime. The fact is you spend about 95 percent of your time thinking about yourself and your problems, and the other 5 percent is spent thinking about things that are getting in the way of you thinking about yourself. Turning off everything in your head (and on your desk) so you become genuinely interested in other people, giving them your undivided attention and really *hearing* them in the midst of a demanding, stressful workplace will be the hardest habit you will ever break. It will require faith that really listening will improve your relationships, income, and career. You have to believe that when you listen, you will build stronger connections with your customers.

You'll also have to overcome the instinct to talk. This requires you to accept that the reason you talk, instead of listening, is because it makes you feel important. Internalize this: It is listening that makes you important in your customer's eyes.

Active Listening

I'll bet my paycheck that you've heard the term *active listening*. Almost everyone in business has attended at least one training session during which she was taught a module on active listening. Active listening is essentially a set of behaviors that are designed to demonstrate to the other person that you are listening. We've already established that the fastest and most effective way to connect with other people is to listen to them because listening makes them feel important. If you want to make them feel unimportant and lose that connection, all you need to do is leave them with the perception that you are not listening. With this in mind, active listening behaviors will serve you well.

Active listening behaviors include making eye contact, acknowledging with verbal feedback and body language, summarizing and restating what you have heard, and utilizing pauses and silence before speaking. The misnomer with active listening is that by practicing these behaviors you will actually *be* listening. It is completely possible to go through the motions of actively listening but not really hear a thing. Note, though, that acting like you are listening is far better than having the other person feel that you are not listening. At least they walk away from the meeting feeling valued and that you care. Turning listening into an emotional connection, however, requires you to actually listen, which means, in addition to demonstrating that you are listening with active listening behaviors, you also have to remove all other distractions, including your own self-centered thoughts, and give the other person your complete attention.

Focusing completely on the person in front of you and being genuinely interested in what they are saying is a learned behavior. Before each meeting, make a commitment to yourself to turn off your own thoughts, desires, and impatience and place all of your attention on the other person. You may even have to say it out loud and prepare yourself mentally to remain focused on the other person. Be aware of your urge to blurt out your idea or tune out other people when you find them boring. Once you are aware of these behaviors, it will be much easier to self-correct. After each conversation, evaluate how well you paid attention, acknowledge your shortcomings, and renew your commitment. When you do this consistently, you will find that listening becomes easier.

Eye Contact

Where the eyes go, so go the ears. Controlling your self-centered thoughts is the key to being there mentally. Controlling your eyes keeps you there physically. Wherever you point your eyes is what you will concentrate on. Practice maintaining good eye contact at all times. Whether face to face or on the phone, avoid the burning desire to multitask by keeping your eyes off papers, computer screens, and cell phones. Turn your electronics off so that beeps, dings, and buzzes don't cause you to look away.

The moment you make the mistake of looking away, you'll not only lose concentration, but you will offend the other person. One trick I use is to look at the other person's eyes and make a note of their eye color. When I do this, it forces me to make solid and genuine eye contact in the critical, first few seconds of a conversation. Eye contact shows others that you are listening. It is also a key to truly connecting with another person. The eyes show emotion and have an amazing way of transmitting empathy.

Listen Deeply

Eye contact, though central to listening, only plays a part. Tim Sanders, author of *The Likeability Factor*, coined the term *listening deeply* to describe listening as an eyes, ears, and heart experience. In other words, watch their body language and expression; analyze the tone, timbre, and pace of their voice; hear their words; and step into their shoes empathically. Since people communicate with far more than words, opening up your other senses affords you the opportunity to analyze the emotional nuances of the conversation. Listening deeply shows other people that you *get* them and naturally draws you closer and strengthens your connection.

When you listen deeply, you are looking for emotional cues, verbal and nonverbal, that open the door to relevant follow-up questions, which lubricate the conversation by keeping the other person talking. It is easy to keep people engaged when they are talking about themselves and their problems. Follow-up questions also allow you to employ the active listening behaviors of summarizing and restating, which show that you are listening, without making statements.

Unlike statements, which tend to stall conversations, questions keep them flowing. Questions also slow down the pace and allow you to clarify your understanding, which is very important for uncovering problems and opportunities to help your customers. Never forget that the more other people are talking, the more connected they feel to you.

Keep Them Talking

There are other active listening behaviors that help you keep conversations moving. Supporting phrases—like "Yes, I see," "I understand," "That's exciting," and so on—keep the other person talking and show that you are listening. Likewise, behaviors like nodding your head and smiling in approval and leaning forward when you find something they say particularly interesting demonstrate that you are listening.

The value of listening in account management is that the more customers talk, the more they trust you. The more they trust, the more they will reveal about their real problems, needs, and wants. When you understand their real problems and how to solve them, you become a valuable resource to them. This is why it is so important to keep them talking.

One sure way to kill a conversation is to blurt out your next question or statement or, worse, talk over your customer before she has finished talking. This makes it transparent that you are not listening, but rather formulating the next thing you plan to say. When you think the other person has finished speaking, pause and count to two before speaking again. This affords you time to fully digest what you have heard before responding. Most importantly, it leaves room for the other person to finish speaking and prevents you from cutting her off if she has not.

The longer you maintain a relationship, the more connected you will be to your client. You will find it easier to initiate and engage in conversations, and those conversations will be more comfortable and revealing. However, nurturing connections requires vigilance.

No matter how long you have known the other person or how comfortable you feel with them, you must always remember to give them your complete attention and listen. Make an effort to avoid talking about yourself and focus on making them feel appreciated and important. Seek out opportunities to compliment and praise their accomplishments. Learn and remember the names of their spouses and children and make note of and acknowledge special days like birthdays, anniversaries, graduations, weddings, and other events that are important to them. Doing so demonstrates with tangible evidence that you are genuinely interested in them and their needs, and that you value and appreciate them.

Remember and Use Names

Remembering and using names when you greet others and in conversations plays an important role in maintaining connections. The one word we respond to and long to hear above all others is our own name. When we are called by name, we feel valued and acknowledged. It sounds beautiful to us. When you remember and use the names of secretaries, security guards, influencers, and others in your customers' accounts, you instantly win them to your cause.

Forget about the old excuse, "I'm terrible with names." You cannot afford the luxury of this excuse. Failing to remember names or mispronouncing names diminishes your likability, breaks connections, and harms your reputation. Frankly, most people don't remember names because remembering names requires work. It is easier to be lazy. Being terrible with names is a choice. *Choose* to develop a system to remember names. You'll find thousands of worthwhile articles and videos with tips on how to remember names with just a quick search on Google. Taking time to read these articles and review the tips is worthwhile. You will find though, that the common threads running across all these resources are the following tips:

Commitment: Deciding and remaining committed to have the self-discipline to remember names. (This is not much different than making the commitment to listen.) Commitment is a choice only you can make.

Concentration: Paying attention when someone says his or her name. This means really listening to the name and how it is pronounced. In other words, you have to be there. If you miss

the name, don't let the moment pass without asking the person
to tell it to you again.

Repetition: Repeating the name to yourself until you seal it into
your memory.

Association: Associating the name with something else that is
easier to remember. A place, company, sound, idea, visual cue,
and so forth.

I have a good friend who seems to have the uncanny ability to
remember the name of every person he has ever met. At first glance,
it appears to be some sort of magic, but on closer observation, his
secret is revealed. The technique he uses, not just for names, but also
for remembering events and subjects of conversations, is to immediately make a note of important things to remember and associate
with the person he met. He just makes his notes right on the back
of their business card. He then enters this information, without
fail, in greater detail into his customer relationship management
(CRM) program at the close of each day before his memory fades.
Then, he reviews the information again the following morning to
ensure he has remembered the name and associated it to the person.
He has more friends than anyone I know.

Remembering and using names is a win-win way to initiate
and maintain connections. It will make you more likable, burnish
your reputation, and make it easy for people to buy you.

Effective Use of E-Mail in Delivering Customer Experience

E-mail is fast, easy, and a primary channel for dealing with customers. It is also a fast and easy way to damage your customer
relationships. It happens daily; account managers with the best of
intentions cause great offense with a simple e-mail message. Making
things worse is the fact that e-mails can be easily forwarded, which

further harms your reputation within your accounts and stokes the emotional fire.

Sometimes a simple misunderstanding of the intent of an e-mail or text message is the spark that ignites a war, which in the blink of an eye, ruins a relationship. It all starts out innocently enough. One party sends a message to another in the attempt to communicate a frustration, concern, want, or need. The receiving party reads the message and becomes offended by the tone. That party then fires back a response (without thinking), which offends the original sender. This exchange of fire continues until both parties, exasperated, are so angry that not only does the original issue go unresolved, but the two parties are often unable to work amicably with each other again. The biggest fights and relationship disintegrations I have witnessed in recent years have been the result of e-mail exchanges.

The major problem with e-mail and text messages is that the person on the other end can't see or hear you. Interpersonal communication is a combination of words, tone of voice, timbre and inflection, body language, and facial expression. When people are unable to associate the words they are reading with the context of your tone and facial expressions, they assign their own meaning to the emotions they read into your words. This is why there is rampant miscommunication with e-mail, text messaging, and at a growing level, social networking tools. These communication tools, while important and useful, are extremely dangerous to customer relationships and can create a bad customer experience in a blink of an eye. They can, however, be managed to your advantage by following some simple rules:

Never express negative emotions. Never express negative emotions like frustration, anger, disappointment, exasperation, or sarcasm. Never criticize—even if the other person has asked for your critique. Negative emotions and criticisms should only be dealt with live, either on the phone or in person.

Express positive emotions. E-mail, voice mail, and text messaging are fantastic tools for praising, complimenting, and expressing gratitude. With these tools you can instantly make people feel valued, important, and appreciated—an excellent way to strengthen connections.

Just give the facts. E-mail is a perfect tool for answering questions, scheduling meetings, and sending information. Used in this manner, it is an asset that allows you to get more done in less time.

Never give bad news or say *no* via e-mail or text. This is very important. When you have bad news to give a customer or you need to deny a request or tell them no, do it live. This gives you the opportunity to let them down gently, explain nuances, and discuss other options.

Avoid negotiating via e-mail. There are times when negotiating via e-mail may be appropriate. However, like bad news, it is difficult to communicate nuance in writing.

Pause before pushing **Send.** Once you push *Send*, you cannot get your message back. Few of us have not experienced regret over a message we sent in haste. Develop the discipline to pause before hitting *Send* (this is especially important if you are on the receiving end of a message that has pissed you off and you are about to fire back a response). Before you send a message, check the tone to ensure that you are expressing either positive emotions or facts. Proofread your e-mails and text messages and play your voice mails back to be sure your message is professional and easy to understand. Stand in the receiver's shoes and consider how you would feel if you were on the receiving end of the message. *Never, ever, ever* send a message when you are angry or frustrated. When in this state, resist the temptation to send a message and come back to it at another time. You'll be amazed at how different things look when you pause.

When in doubt, pick up the phone. The most effective way to communicate is in real time. No matter how brilliant you believe your communication skills are, you cannot win an argument or carry on a conversation via e-mail. You will always do more harm than good attempting to clarify misunderstandings with messaging tools. When you sense frustration, need to convey negative emotion or criticism, or are looking for clarification, pick up the phone and make a call. In virtually all cases, a short phone call clears things up and leaves both parties feeling heard, appreciated, and understood. If you want to use messaging tools to your advantage, practice this rule before pushing *Send*. If there is even a slight bit of doubt about how your message will be received and interpreted, pick up the phone.

6 | Solve Problems

"When I started working with this customer four years ago, we were splitting the business with several competitors. They had plants across the country and I wanted them all, but my customer felt like they were better off not putting all of their eggs in one basket." Mitch, a national account manager assigned to a large food account, explained "Recently, though, we were awarded an exclusive contract for all of their business."

Mitch is a problem solver. He works relentlessly to understand his clients' businesses and proactively bring solutions to the table. This customer is a huge national food manufacturer and his focus has been helping them reduce expenses.

"Every customer is different and they have different needs. In this case, their margins were getting squeezed so I went on the hunt for every opportunity to pull cost out of the business. I could see that the stakeholders in this account had way too much on their plates so I did my best to focus on what was most important to them and at the same time reduce their administrative burden."

Armed with data and reports, he took the lead with his corporate level contact to arrange meetings with plant managers and other stakeholders at the locations that he serviced. He set up cost baselines and showed them how they could use his service to avoid expenses and reduce waste in their operations. He focused on win-win strategies that created value for his customer and his company. The word started getting out about Mitch and his cost saving ideas. The other plant managers—the ones served by his competitors—wanted to talk, too.

He was also making his corporate buyer look good. "The numbers were starting to add up into the millions of dollars in savings. It was getting noticed and my corporate contact was looking good to her boss. When you help your buyers and contacts look good, they will help you. My corporate buyer started pushing the other plants to look at our service offering and one by one I started picking them off. This year I finally got the exclusive contract."

This is not a single instance for Mitch. As a national account manager, his role is to manage the account relationships and grow his base of business by finding opportunity within the accounts. He employs a similar process in each of his accounts to proactively find and solve problems. In another case, he was given a new account from the sales team with only 5 of the 50 locations signed. He developed so much trust with the buyer that he was awarded the other locations just a year later.

The buyers Mitch works with love him. They openly used those words when I interviewed them. The reason they love him: *"He is constantly looking for a way to help me."* Mitch has garnered tremendous respect from his customers because he is a problem solver. His career is flourishing, too. He is well respected within his company and consistently crushes his plan—earning him big bonuses and raises.

When you strip everything else away—the myriad customer service philosophies, the clichés, marketing slogans, technology, and so on—customer service and account management is about one thing: *One person (You) helping another person (Your Customer) solve a problem. Otherwise, what is the point?* You can build the most connected relationships ever; you can employ sophisticated customer service processes and techniques; your company can invest in the latest technology for managing customer relationships and issues; you can deploy sophisticated strategic account management processes; and your marketing team can create cool slogans that attempt to sell your company's focus on the customer. None of this matters, however, if *you* are not solving your customers' problems. Frankly, if you want a cool slogan to remind you about what it takes to make customers love you, write this on a piece of paper and hang it up where you will see it every day: *It's Problem Solving, Stupid.*

Customers don't meet with you, call, e-mail, text, or track you down on social media just to chew the fat. Think about your own experience over the past month or poll other account managers. How many customers, out of the blue, called just to say, "Wow you are doing a great job! That's all I wanted to say."? How many called just to hang out and ask you about your family or weekend? They didn't. Your customers are crazy busy. No different than you. They are working hard to keep their businesses and departments running, serve their customers, and stay employed. Customers are not calling unless they need help solving a problem.

Solving problems is the foundation of the *People Love You* philosophy. The fact is, people become emotionally attached to people who solve their problems. Just ask Mitch's buyers. Consider for a moment people in your own life—personal or business—who have helped you solve a problem. As you see these people in your mind or remember what they did for you, it is likely that you feel an emotional connection to them. You may even feel that *you owe them one.*

Solving problems is about helping your customers get what they want. When you help your customers get what they want, you will get what you want. For example, when you help your client solve a business problem with your product or service, they may be more willing to recommend you to someone else, they may buy more from you, and they will be less willing to entertain offers from your competitors.

Problem Solvers Are the Champions of the Business World

Glen was seated in the front row of an audience I was speaking to in Tampa, Florida. Right in the middle of my speech I saw his hand go up. This wasn't a give and take kind of presentation. It was a large room and I'd been hired to do a keynote and do it within a set time frame. At first I ignored him. But when I turned back to his side of the room his hand was still up. What could I do?

As I walked toward him, he stood up and said loudly, "I want to tell you that what you are saying about problem solvers is true." He reached for my microphone and before I could pull it back, he had it in his hand and was talking to the audience. He introduced himself as the CFO of a glass manufacturing company. I prayed that he would be brief.

He told a story about an account manager named Terry who worked for one of his vendors. "A couple of years ago we were having a big problem with the turning radius on some of our forklifts and hand trucks. Terry overheard our managers talking about it and offered to help. Terry explained that another one of his customers had experienced a similar issue and he could connect us with someone who could help us fix our problem. The next day Terry made a personal introduction and shortly after, our problem was solved."

Then Glen delivered the punch line: The service Terry provided had nothing to do with forklifts or warehouses. Terry worked to solve a problem that wasn't even his. He just saw an issue his customer was having and jumped in to help. "We love this guy," Glen explained. "Whenever he is in our plant, he is totally focused on us. He spends time on the line, in the warehouse, and with our managers and is always looking for ways to help us. I can tell you that when Terry's competitors come knocking, we send them away. As long as Terry is there, his company will never have to worry about losing their account with us." Then he handed back the microphone and sat down. I looked around at the audience. They got it. Glen's story was perfect and it hammered home my point that people and companies are extremely loyal and emotionally attached to people who solve their problems.

Problem solvers are the champions of the business world and customer magnets. When you actively and consistently solve problems, customers view you as a resource they can't live without. Your customers will pull you in as a resource during planning and strategic meetings, giving you an opportunity to influence and improve their business by helping them solve even more problems. The more problems you solve, the more they love you, and you will have little trouble engaging them in conversations about contract renewals, new business opportunities, upsells, and even rate increases.

Here is the good news: Your customers have problems. When you roll up your sleeves and get in there with them to help solve those problems, your competitors don't have a chance.

Problem Solving Starts with Who You Are— Not What You Do

Mitch, from our opening story, works in a very difficult industry, where virtually all of the competitor products are the same. Mitch must rely on local service teams to take care of his customers and execute the service programs he creates that solve his customers' problems. Due to cutbacks, he doesn't get a lot of support and has little budget to work with. His product and service are flawed. Yet, his customers love him and he is growing his accounts. Mitch's customers do business with Mitch. They love *him* because he proactively solves their problems.

Problem solving is a character trait. It is an internal belief and value system that manifests itself outwardly through your actions. There is no doubt that some people are more gifted as problem solvers than others. They were born with the God-given talent for serving others. These lucky few don't have to work as hard as the rest of us to hone the *problem solver* character trait.

Just because you are not a *born* problem solver does not mean you cannot develop the skill. Of course, like many human relationship skills, the process of solving problems is simple. Actually doing it is the hard part. It starts with internalizing problem solving as your core philosophy. This is a conscious decision that only *you* can make. It is a decision to let go of your agenda and your needs and wants, and instead focus your time, attention, and emotion on serving others. It is a decision to put your customer first. Effective problem solving requires you to develop the skills for:

- Questioning
- Listening
- Project management
- Follow-up
- Follow-through
- Leveraging resources

Most important is developing awareness. Like Terry, from the previous story, you must hone the skill of awareness so that you are always focused on and looking for problems you can solve. Much of the work in developing this skill is learning how to suppress your natural human desire to focus on what you want and shifting that energy to a focus on what is important for your customer.

Empathy is the mother of awareness. "Some people think only intellect counts: knowing how to solve problems, knowing how to get by, knowing how to identify an advantage and seize it. But the functions of intellect are insufficient without . . . empathy." I've quoted author Dean Koontz's words regarding empathy in all of the books in this series because quite honestly, I haven't found a better, more concise way to express how fundamental empathy is in problem solving.

Empathy is the ability to step into someone else's shoes and see things from their perspective. It is the ability to understand and identify with another's feelings or motives. It is looking at problems through their eyes. This is where awareness is born and where it develops.

True awareness requires intellect and empathy. Both play vital roles in relationships, communication, and problem solving. Empathy gives you insight into your customer's needs, wants, fears, and desires. It helps you overcome the habit of viewing the landscape through only your perspective and assuming you know what is best. It helps you see each person as a unique individual. Problem solvers understand that regardless of how common a problem may be, each person views her own problems as special.

It is standing in your customer's shoes and viewing problems from their perspective that allows you to tap into your intellect to leverage resources and execute plans that deliver personalized solutions to problems. These personalized solutions connect with your customer emotionally. They are the key to building trust, gaining more business, long-term customer retention, and delivering a legendary customer experience.

Five Rules of Questioning

Questions are the gateway to problem solving. Learning and practicing effective questioning skills is central to success in virtually every facet of business. Questioning (and, of course, listening) is critical when dealing with customers and solving problems. Effective questions give you a window into what your customer is thinking and how they are feeling. Questions peel away layers of miscommunication that often obscure the real problem. And questions, asked the right way, demonstrate empathy and help you remain emotionally connected to your customer.

Before we dive deeper into questioning strategies, I want to explain five rules of questioning. These rules will guide you in asking the right questions, at the right time, in the right way.

Rule 1: People Won't Tell You Their Real Problems until They Feel Connected to You

We covered this extensively in the last chapter. With account management, this rule comes into play on two levels.

Proactive. First, as an account manager, part of your job may be to grow your base of business by adding services, upselling, getting rate increases, or increasing orders. These opportunities for growth are built on a foundation of proactive problem solving. That means being aware of opportunities to help your client and asking questions about those opportunities.

Reactive. When customers come to you with problems, you've got to take action to resolve them. This means understanding the real issue and leveraging resources to fix it. When customers call you about a problem, they will sometimes begin the conversation by attacking you or your company. If their actions or inactions created the problem, they will deflect blame or responsibility. Your natural inclination will be to put your emotional wall up to protect yourself or to fight back. Neither of these behaviors leads to effective problem solving.

In either case, customers naturally want to hide their vulnerability. Even with customers where you feel you have the best relationships, it is likely that they have their emotional walls up. This is even more prevalent with new customers or customers with whom you have not established a relationship.

Connecting is designed to pull the wall down. You create the opportunity to connect by relaxing, and remaining open and empathic. You connect by listening, giving people your complete attention, and being genuinely interested in what they have to say.

Rule 2: Ask Easy Questions First

To get people to lower their emotional walls and reveal their problems, you need them to talk. The more they talk, the more problems—and the more about their problems—they will reveal. To make it easy for people to talk, start the conversation off with questions that are easy (without sounding patronizing) for your customer to answer. Once they feel comfortable talking, you can begin asking deeper, more strategic questions that will reveal their real problems and the root causes of those problems.

Rule 3: People Communicate with Stories

In conversations, people don't spit out bullet pointed facts. Instead, they use stories. When you listen attentively, you encourage the speaker to expand on and tell more stories. The clues that lead to their real problems are buried inside these stories.

Of course, this requires patience. In customer service situations, those stores can often sound like run on sentences that will never end. Remember Rule 1? A fast way to lose the emotional connection with a customer is to cut them off mid-sentence when they are telling you their story.

As crazy as this sounds, part of the customer experience is telling you her story, no matter how convoluted it might be. The customer wants to talk—sometimes at you. It makes them feel good to get things off of their chest—even though it feels like they are attacking you.

That is why, virtually every time, if you let an irate customer get it all out while not judging him, snapping back, becoming defensive, or in any way giving him a hint that you are irritated or upset, he will calm down, open up, and very often apologize for his behavior.

What you must never forget is that the clues to solving problems are contained in those stories. *Listen*.

Rule 4: Be Empathetic—Follow Emotional Cues to Problems

Listening deeply with your eyes, ears, and heart will lead you to emotional cues like voice inflection, facial expressions, and body language, which indicate that a story point or issue has emotional significance. When you find these cues, use follow-up questions to dig deeper. This is where real problems and concerns will be revealed.

Rule 5: Never Make Assumptions

Many account managers and customer service professionals assume that they know exactly what the problem is or what their customer needs. Because of this they dump solutions on their customer or worse, ask leading or loaded questions designed to prove their customer wrong. They assume, rather than ask questions, because they are in a hurry, bored, impatient, lack empathy, and in some unfortunate cases, believe their customer is stupid. Besides all of the obvious pitfalls of assuming, there is also an emotional trap. No one—not you, not me, not your customer—likes to be told that he or she is not unique. We resent it. We want to be treated as individuals. The key is to get your customers talking about what they want and need, no matter how obvious the problem.

My anger flared. *I spent almost $30,000 a year with this vendor and they treated me this way!* I'd just spent more than an hour creating screenshots, examples, and detailed reports of an issue we were having with their cloud-based software. This had been my third try to get my account manager's attention. On previous attempts he had quickly sent back *proof* that there was nothing wrong with the system. (He assumed he knew what was going on and did not treat my issue as unique.)

By the time I sent him my detailed report, I was furious. Not so much about the issue—I know software has bugs. Rather, I was furious that he was not listening to me. When he responded to my third e-mail with a screenshot of something not even related to my problem, I knew he wasn't paying any attention. He was focused on proving me wrong rather than solving my problem.

Instead of listening to me and jumping in to understand the issue from my point of view, he focused only on his need to get me off of his back.

Sadly, this happens far too often. Instead of helping customers solve problems, customer service professionals assume they know what is happening and waste time attempting to prove the customer wrong. It is one of the reasons customers are often ready for a fight when they call or write for help.

If you want to provide great customer experiences, don't waste time proving your customers wrong. Instead of assuming that they are wrong, assume that they are right and start troubleshooting. Ask questions, dig deep, and treat their problems with the respect they deserve.

It is true that customers want their problems solved. However, they also want to feel important and to be treated with dignity. They want you to treat *them* and *their problem* like they are unique. When your first response is to prove them wrong or to dismiss them, you wreck your customer's experience. Sometimes you even lose the account. I eventually tired of dealing with the account manager who would not help me solve problems and moved my business to his competitor who was hungry to work with us. By the time he and his manager called to beg us to stay, it was too late.

Look Out for Icebergs

If you've ever had a chance to see an iceberg up close, you know how impressively huge they can be. What is hard to fathom, though, is that the tip of the iceberg is only a small portion of the total mass, which is hidden below the surface. Those who navigate the oceans recognize that it is this hidden mass that poses the greatest danger to their vessels. On ships that sail in seas where icebergs float, there is always someone on lookout. Failure to heed the danger posed by the hidden mass of icebergs leads to disastrous and fatal consequences.

Customers are just like icebergs, often revealing only a fraction of the information you need, while their real problems are hidden from view. Until you get beneath the surface, you have no way of knowing if you are addressing the most important issues for your client.

Consider Amy, an account manager who calls her customer to check in: "Hi Rick, how are you doing? I'm just checking in to see how are things going?"

Rick, the buyer, answers: "I'm super busy right now and can't talk, Amy, but everything is good, thanks for calling."

Comfortable that she has covered "relationship building" with Rick, Amy records the call in her CRM and sets Rick up for a follow-up call in a month. Later that week, when her manager asks her about Rick's account she tells him that all is well. "Yeah, I just spoke with Rick. He's very happy."

Three weeks later, Rick calls Amy. After a quick exchange of pleasantries, Rick explains that he's decided to start buying from one of her competitors and will not need next month's shipment. Stunned, Amy asks why. Rick explains that the other vendor had a better solution to one of his most pressing production line problems—*a problem that Amy knew nothing about*. Amy stammers back, "I just spoke to you and you didn't say anything about that issue. We have the best solution on the market for that problem. I'll get my manager on the phone now and we'll have our engineers over later this week."

But it is too late. The decision has been made. Rick explains that they are going to give the new vendor a try and offers a platitude: "If things don't work out, we'll take a look at your solution."

Amy's ship is sunk. She reluctantly walks to her manager's office to deliver the bad news. Why didn't Amy know about this problem? Simple: She never got below the surface.

Amy is a *just checking in* surface skimmer. She believes falsely that by just checking in, she is building and maintaining relationships. Deep down inside, perhaps subconsciously, she doesn't want to know if there are problems or complaints. She asks superficial questions that allow her to check the relationship box and hide from real problems. Because of this, her customer relationships are superficial.

She explains to her boss that she is dumbfounded that Rick would switch vendors. She cannot understand why he didn't say anything to her about the issue. It makes no sense to her that he would go to all of the trouble to change to a new vendor when she could have quickly solved his problems. "What more could I have done?" she asks her boss.

What she didn't know is that Rick was getting pressure from his production manager (PM) to change. A salesperson from one of Amy's competitors had been calling on the PM and had made a good case to change. Rick knew that it made more sense to keep working with Amy's company, but the PM had been bugging him for months and he just wanted to get the guy off of his back. He'd thought about calling Amy and asking her to send her engineers to talk to the PM, but other priorities had gotten in the way. The easy way out was to just let the production manager have his way.

Customers don't naturally reveal their real problems, needs, and wants. They are not going to easily let you below the surface. They will do things for their reasons, and not yours. If she had developed a real connection with Rick and used that connection to ask deeper, more strategic questions to get below the surface, he may have revealed what was going on and given her an opportunity to address the issue. In all customer relationships, *look out for icebergs.*

Dual Process Questioning

Here is a fact: The more questions you ask, the more problems you will solve. Of course, to solve a problem, you must first uncover the *real* problem. To do that, you ask questions. The reason I continue to repeat this mantra is that most account managers and customer service professionals don't ask enough questions.

You've likely been through some type of training program in which you were taught about open-ended and closed-ended questions. In the training, you learned that open-ended questions are good and closed-ended questions are bad. From there, a few general examples of open-ended questions and closed-ended questions were passed around the training room and, unfortunately, the questioning module was then concluded.

These training programs are effective in teaching you the difference between open- and closed-ended questions, but ineffective in teaching you how to apply questioning skills in the real world. If you were to interview 100 business professionals, 99 of them would tell you that open-ended questions are the most effective questions. However, if you were to observe these same people interacting with customers, you would mostly hear closed-ended and leading questions. Why? Because account managers too often assume that they know what the problem is rather than discovering the problem through open-ended questions.

The most effective problem solvers operate in *dual-process* mode when working with customers. Dual-process means they are able to ask questions that help them uncover and reveal problems while maintaining their emotional connection with the customer. In other words, they remain empathetic—standing in the customer's shoes—while at the same time focusing on their business objective.

To be effective at dual-process questioning, your questions must be engrained in your memory so that you can access them in a nonlinear way, based on the specific situation and client. This is accomplished by becoming an expert in your product or service and how that product or service is applied in your customer's situation. This knowledge is gained through training, self-study, and experience. You must also invest the time to learn about your customers' business situations. One of the top complaints customers have about their account managers is that they don't take time to understand their businesses. If you don't understand your customer's business situation it will be difficult to ask questions that uncover opportunities to help them. The key is dedicating yourself to learning.

You also need to develop both empathy questions and questions relevant to your product or service. *Empathy questions* include easy questions for getting conversations started and *clarifying questions* for checking emotional cues like *worry questions*. Worry questions are excellent tools for getting customers to open up to you about their problems and demonstrating empathy. Questions like: "What worries you about that situation?" or "What concerns you the most about this situation?" are variations.

An inventory of questions that are specifically relevant to your product, service, customer, or industry will help you quickly troubleshoot issues. Unfortunately, most training programs are not going to provide you with a useful list of questions. So this is something you will have to create on your own. The first step is to find out what is already available. It is likely that someone in your organization, at one time or another, created a list of questions.

The next step is interviewing your manager, peers, trainers, and anyone else in your organization who is willing to talk to you. Find out what questions top account managers in your company ask, in which situations, to which people. Are there different variations of the same questions that are more effective than others? Are there situations where you shouldn't ask certain questions? What are the anticipated answers? This discovery process will aid you in developing a comprehensive list. Then build your list. Organize it into sections that make it easy to find questions based on your customer's situation. Write the questions out the way you would say them—in your own style. Be sure to include possible follow-up questions.

Finally, practice. The only true way to become competent with dual-process questioning is to practice on real customers in real time. Yes, it will be awkward at first and you will make mistakes. You'll assume. You'll focus on the next question instead of listening to your client. You'll frustrate them with irrelevant questions, which demonstrate that you have not invested the time to understand their business.

Trust me, I have been there. I've stumbled on my words, made embarrassing mistakes, and sounded like a robot. I've frustrated and made customers mad in the process. By sticking with it, day in and day out, though, dual-process questioning became second nature. I did not have to think as hard, and I started sounding authentic. Soon, I knew what to ask in just about any situation, including follow-up questions and I was able to troubleshoot and solve difficult problems while maintaining connections with my customers.

Proactive Problem Solving Is the Key

Vijay had built a solid relationship with his contact, Evan, who was the director of fixed operations for a national car dealership group. They'd become good friends along the way and usually got in a round of golf when Vijay visited. While waiting on the ninth tee box for the group ahead, Vijay made a light joke about being Evan's favorite account manager. To Vijay's surprise, Evan deadpanned, "Actually, Linda is my best account manager. She's always one step ahead of me. No matter what I'm thinking, she's already there." Linda was an account manager for one of Vijay's competitors. They shared the service contract for Evan's dealerships. "That hurt!" said Vijay. "At first I just blew it off but the more I thought about it, I knew I had to change. I needed to get more proactive with my approach if I wanted to stand out with Evan and pick up more of his business."

It is a powerful statement, and you retain more control when you anticipate problems and bring solutions to the table before your customers ask for them. Smart account managers are constantly analyzing each of their customers and developing solutions designed to help those customers deal with their unique problems. For large, strategic customers, they build strategic business plans. This proactive approach not only ensures long-term customer retention, but it opens the door to account growth because it demonstrates to your customers that you care and are a valued partner.

Why is this so important? When you proactively tackle problems, customers see you at your best. You are perceived as a confident professional who understands their unique business issues. You also save your customers time and relieve them of their overwhelming workload. You also position them to win with their bosses, internal stakeholders, and company.

Meredith, like many of the top account managers we interviewed, schedules regular account reviews with her large clients. "When I first started setting up these reviews they were mostly a look back on what we had done in the account: service issues, cost over runs, quality problems, and things like that. After about a year, I realized that the meetings had become stale and boring and all we were doing was spending time rehashing the past and pointing out what was wrong. It was like trying to swim in quicksand. I was working hard but getting nowhere and I felt like these meetings were just opportunities for my customers to beat me up."

So Meredith changed her approach. "After taking some advice from one of my peers, I began walking into these meetings with a plan for the future. Yeah, we still talked about past issues, but the dialogue changed. We began talking about ways we could innovate and how I could help my customers achieve their business goals. The conversations were more robust and I worked hard to bring real solutions and recommendations to each meeting. My customers liked it better and I walked away from those meetings feeling more confident and better about myself."

Meredith told me how, over time, she became a trusted advisor for many of her customers. They began pulling her into strategy sessions to get her opinion. Conversations about contract extensions began earlier and were less tense. Her customers viewed her as a resource they could not live without and Meredith found it easier to retain her customer base.

The Pull Strategy—Becoming a Trusted Advisor

One of my clients is a well-known and respected defense contractor. For years, the renewal of their government contracts was a given. Because they were so embedded within the fabric of the defense department and other governmental agencies, it was too hard or too much work to switch to another supplier. In other cases, they were the only game in town. Life was good. With their customers locked into long-term contracts that were effectively guaranteed to renew, managers had no motivation to focus on relationships and proactive problem solving.

However, during the economic downturn that hit hard in 2008 and the subsequent political gridlock, things changed rapidly. Governmental agencies, driven by politics and a focus on cost cutting, began scrutinizing contracts more closely. At the same time, smaller and more nimble entrepreneurial competitors began to win contracts that for years had been considered untouchable. Suddenly, every contract was at risk and company executives woke up to the value of relationships. The stakes were huge—literally billions of dollars were on the line.

The company has two critical imperatives with each contract. They need to retain the contract when it goes out for bid and they need to grow the revenue of each account by providing additional services as add-ons to current contracts. Their account managers, manage both the team responsible for the account and the relationship with their customer. Failure to renew their contract can and often does cost the program manager and their staff their jobs.

As more contracts were lost to competitors and cost cutting, there was an awakening within the executive ranks that they needed to change the way their program managers were engaging customers. Upon taking a closer look at the data, they discovered that some program managers, in the midst of intense competitive pressure and budget cuts, were generating significant growth within their programs, winning contract renewals, and locking out their competitors.

A task group was created to discover what these successful program managers were doing right and thereby develop best practices that could be taught across the enterprise. The task force discovered a common thread among the successful PMs: They had become an actual extension of their customers. Customers viewed the successful PMs as strategic resources and pulled them into meetings, relied on them as experts and advisors who helped solve problems, and trusted them as advocates who worked on behalf of the customer within their organization. Because these PMs had established such a foundation of trust with their customers and become such an integral part of the customer's team, they had the unique ability to influence and shape their customer's decisions.

It is important that you understand that in order to become a trusted advisor, the successful program managers left their personal agendas at the door. They understood that in order to win their customer's trust, to be consistently pulled in by their customer, they had to be focused on their customer's unique needs and issues. To become an extension of the customer, they had to leave their own wants and needs behind.

I realize that this may seem counterintuitive given the fact that their objective (much like your objectives) was to grow their program, make it more profitable, and renew the contract. Clearly, they did not lose sight of their responsibilities to achieve those objectives. However, they achieved these objectives where others failed because they approached issues from their customer's standpoint rather than from their own.

It is the spirit in which you approach problem solving that matters most. When you truly put your own needs and wants aside, customers reward you with trust and lean on you more and more for help and advice. Not long ago, one of my largest customers pulled us into an all-day strategic meeting to discuss sales talent sourcing strategies and how they could improve their processes. The customer also asked five of our competitors to attend the meeting.

Frankly, as we all filed into the meeting room and took our seats, it was uncomfortable. Each account manager sized up the other competitors. As the facilitator (a neutral consultant) posed questions and engaged the group, the account managers who had come to the meeting with their own selfish agendas stood out like sore thumbs. Their answers and dialogue centered on what was important to them and what they wanted rather than on our client's problems. They were boring and self-serving, and our customer was not impressed.

This customer went on to pull us together for subsequent meetings and discussions. However, they did not invite the self-centered account managers. The group that was invited was given the opportunity to help our customer shape their future strategy and we were rewarded with more business and opportunity at the expense of those who were shut out.

A simple way to put your agenda aside is when you are with a customer, instead of focusing on how you and your company do things, ask your customers about how *they* do things. Do *questions* (and obvious variations) help you remain focused on what is important to your customer, learn more about them, and open up dialogue that helps your customer discuss their real problems:

- I've done some research on (this process, product, department, etc.). Can you tell me more about what you do here?
- How do you do that?
- Why do you do it that way?

- Where do you (produce, service, manufacture, ship) this?
- How does that work?
- Are there other ways you do that?
- Can you tell me more about what that new product you are manufacturing does?
- Who does that?

Since people tend to communicate in stories, listen deeply to pick up unsaid feelings and emotions. Watch for facial expressions, body language, and voice tonality that offer clues to underlying importance. You don't have to be an expert in body language to see obvious clues. You only need to be observant and prepared to ask follow-up questions to test your hunch like, "That sounds pretty important. How are you dealing with it?"

Listening and asking follow-up questions makes the other person feel important, creates a deeper feeling of connection, and opens access to the emotions and problems that lie below the surface. It is at this point that your questions may become more focused, specific, and relevant to your overriding business objectives. This dual-process questioning is the key to getting below the surface and identifying their *real* problems.

Dual-process questioning is nonlinear in nature. It is designed to be fluid, flexible, and open to multiple avenues of questioning that access your customer's emotions and provide a clearer picture of the problems, pitfalls, and issues that lie below the surface. Using fluid, dual-process questioning allows you the flexibility to adjust your questions strategically as you uncover the problems that are most emotional and pressing to your customer.

Many account managers use a linear questioning process. They go through a checklist of questions that help them gather just enough information to pitch their product or service. To gain your customer's trust it is important that you resist the temptation to pitch your product or service at every opportunity. Your customer will be reticent to pull you in as an extension of their team if they feel like you are just going to dump your product or company information on them at every turn. Trust me on this point. You will sell far more to your customer by asking questions and listening rather than pitching. You become a trusted advisor by maintaining an acute attention on your customer and their business.

Connecting Problems to Solutions

Presenting solutions to your customers' problems is a process and a key part of delivering a great customer experience. To be treated as a trusted advisor requires you to present solutions that articulate, verbally and in writing, how you, your strategy, and your product or service will solve each problem. You need to show your customer how your solution will create value or benefit them. This is how you bridge your product or service to your customer's problem, and present your recommendations to your customer. The process that works best for this is as follows:

1. **Articulate your customer's unique problem:** Mary, in human resources, is spending 30 hours a week on payroll-related issues. This is keeping her from managing benefits enrollment.
2. **Recommend a solution:** We recommend implementing HR Pro 1000 software package, which will fully automate your payroll process.
3. **Show them the planned result (value):** Mary will be free to spend her time enrolling employees in the benefits plan, which will save you $22,000 a year in part-time labor and improve morale.

Once you know your customer's problems, it should be fairly easy to develop solutions. Sometimes you may need to get creative, but in most cases the problems are the same ones many of your customers have. Never forget however, that each person sees his or her problems, no matter how common, as unique. For this reason your presentation of *recommended solutions* and *planned results* must be personalized. You must articulate it in a way that makes your customer feel that the solution is special and specific to them. Always tie your recommendations and value statements back to the emotional hot buttons they revealed during questioning. The impact of this is tremendous, because once again your customer will feel listened to, valued, and important.

Connecting the Dots with Account Management Process

Take a moment and imagine that you are standing in a 20 × 20 room. Look around at the walls. Covering every inch of the walls and ceilings are dartboards. A man walks in through a hidden door and hands you a box of darts. His instructions are to pick a dartboard and throw a dart. He tells you that if you hit the dartboard, you'll get a prize.

You think to yourself, *Dude this is easy. There are dartboards everywhere.* So you pick a target and throw the dart. Bull's-eye! You pump your fist and celebrate. A few minutes later the man walks in and says, "No prize for you! That was the wrong dartboard. Try again."

So you throw a dart and hit another bull's-eye. Again, you pump your fist and celebrate. After some time, the man walks in and informs you that you hit the wrong board. No prize for you!

Several rounds later you get a little smarter and ask the man, "Which boards should I aim to hit?" The man says, "Only the right ones."

So you ask which ones are the right ones. The man says, "Why are you asking me this? You are a professional; you should know." So you aim at another wall and release a dart.

The man walks back into the room and looks disapprovingly at your dart embedded in the target and says, "Wrong target. No prize for you!"

By now you are getting frustrated. So you demand, "If you don't tell me which targets to aim at, I'm quitting!" Reluctantly, he points to the far wall and tells you to try over there.

You take aim, throw the dart, and hit a target. Then you wait and wait and wait—afraid to celebrate. Several hours later the man comes back in. He takes a quick look at your dart and shakes his head. "No prize for you!"

Now you are pissed. "Look here!" you shout. "You said I should aim over there. I did that, and now you are telling me that it is still not good enough. What the hell do you want from me?!"

The man says, "Are you stupid? I've already told you I only want you to hit the right ones. What part of right don't you get?" He storms out of the room.

You are steaming mad. You call him vile names and scream that this whole thing is unfair. Finally, after you have figured out that you can't win, you leave and never come back.

If this scenario sounds ridiculous to you, don't be quick to dismiss it as *too dramatic* or *not probable*. This is what it is like to chase customer expectations when you have failed to establish performance targets and metrics with your customer upfront and on an ongoing basis. Too often, account managers assume they know what customers want based on their internal company standards, what makes other customers happy, or their own internal compass.

You may think you know what your customer wants or expects but I remind you that customers do things for their reasons, and not yours. Each customer has a unique expectation for the ROI they get from your product or service based on their business situation and experience, which, by the way, is based on what is most important to them—not you. If you don't know what that ROI is for each customer, you'll spend your time chasing your tail. You will also have a difficult time shaping your customers' expectations should they be or become unrealistic.

If the ultimate goal of account management and customer service is to help your customers win by solving their problems, doesn't it make sense to know what winning means to them? If your account is going in the wrong direction or you find yourself chasing shifting customer expectations, it is likely you don't know what the target is because you haven't asked your customer to clearly articulate the ROI they expect. A key part of your account management process must be establishing performance targets and metrics for each customer.

We should not forget that account management is a process. Put simply, a process is a repeatable set of steps that, when followed, lead to your strategic or tactical objective. Each touch point in that process impacts customer experience. As the complexity and size of the account increases, so do the sub-steps and the number of people involved in the account on both the customer and company sides.

There are dozens of popular account management systems. Many large companies have their own proprietary strategic or key account management process. My company helps organizations develop account management and customer service systems. Which one is best? My answer is always the same, "The one that works for you." Some of the key elements of an effective account management process include:

- Strategic Account Plan
- Account Goals and Objectives
- Account Contact Map (key contacts and influencers inside your account)
- Internal Roles and Responsibilities
- Call and Visitation Schedule and Frequency
- Reporting (internal and external) Process and Frequency
- Account Review Process
- Contract Renewal Process
- Executive Level Account Involvement
- CRM Management

Far too many account managers operate without a systematic process for developing and maintaining relationships with customers. Their approach is often random and chaotic. In the absence of a disciplined account management process, they have the tendency to focus on low ROI activities while neglecting more important customer touch points that shape customer experience.

Though the account management process and elements will differ based on the size and strategic importance of the account, the importance of following a disciplined, structured, and systematic process for managing your accounts remains the same. Your account management process is where all the touch points that impact customer experience intersect. It is the fulcrum on which the *Five Levers of Customer Experience* pivot, helping you develop deep, enduring relationships with your customers and deliver legendary customer experiences.

7

Build Trust

When I first met Lonnie, he reminded me of Billy Bob Thornton's character, Karl Childress, in the movie *Sling Blade*. Lonnie, a country boy from South Carolina, spoke deliberately and only when there was something that "needed to be said." Otherwise, he was all business.

Lonnie serviced a portfolio of 120 business customers valued at around $520,000 in annual revenue. His customer base ranged from heavy manufacturing to service-based companies. He'd been with his company for 22 years and had been the number one route service rep (RSR) in the Southeast region (out of 220 RSRs) each year for the past 14 years, earning annual president's club trips to Hawaii for him and his wife. For six consecutive years, he had retained 100 percent of his customer base. A retention level that was unheard of in his industry, which is notorious for poor service and unhappy customers. (The average customer retention rate in his region was 86.1 percent; at his location, it was barely 80 percent.) One hundred percent customer retention in this industry was impossible—except that Lonnie had achieved the impossible.

The location where Lonnie works (called a *depot*) is a union shop and Lonnie is a member of the union. The Teamsters fiercely protect the RSRs there from disciplinary action, stemming from providing subpar customer service. The management team at Lonnie's depot is dysfunctional at best. They spend the vast majority of their time at war with the union and, out of spite, frustration, or both, provide little support to the RSRs. Making things worse, the company's systems and processes for service delivery are antiquated and broken. Yet, within this less than desirable culture, Lonnie delivers an extraordinary level of service, day in and day out. Despite all of the roadblocks, Lonnie's customers love him.

To learn what makes Lonnie special, I spent three days shadowing him on his route. I first met Lonnie on the loading dock at 4 a.m.—three hours earlier than the official starting time at the depot. Lonnie was already busy at work. I asked him why he got started so early in the morning (I was wondering myself what had possessed me to get up in the dark). He said that by getting there early he was able to do a complete inventory, allowing him to replace missing items and make a note to discuss with his customer in the event that he could not find a replacement that day. He explained that a major reason for dissatisfaction in his industry was caused by missing items from the weekly deliveries. Lonnie took great care to organize his truck so that he had no trouble finding what he needed for each delivery. Most RSRs didn't take the time to build an organized load. That, he said, made them inefficient, leaving them less time to spend face-to-face with each customer.

Once his truck was loaded, he sat down and meticulously went over all of his notes from previous deliveries, reviewed each invoice for accuracy, and reviewed customer service calls from the previous day. Then he went through a final checklist to be sure he had everything he needed to serve his customers. It reminded me of the check process pilots go through before take-off.

We pulled out of the parking lot at 6 a.m. (long before the other RSRs would arrive). Our first stop was Krispy Kreme. My mouth watered as we walked in. The smell of fresh doughnuts and coffee filled the place. But Lonnie wasn't there for a morning pick-me-up. He walked right up to the counter where a clerk named Lester greeted him with a smile and a stack of boxes filled with freshly cooked doughnuts. We loaded them in his truck and headed off in the early dawn. "Lonnie, what are these doughnuts for?"

"You'll see," he replied stoically.

Our first stop was at a huge manufacturing operation that fabricated metal products. Inside, the plant was hot from smelting pots. Men and women in hard hats and thick gloves worked with large pieces of steel and iron. The smell of burning metal and oil permeated everything. As Lonnie walked onto the production floor, with me in tow, people looked up, waved, and smiled. "Hey Lonnie," one after another called out.

Lonnie dropped the fresh donuts off at various places in the plant and took a box into the office where he greeted one of several departmental heads he worked with. They were smiling and Lonnie was smiling. Lonnie, the stoic, *Sling Blade*-like character, had suddenly become animated and gregarious. He greeted the people in the plant by name. He genuinely loved his customers and they loved him right back.

As I helped him with his deliveries, he explained that this was his largest customer and a prime target for his competitors' salespeople. He did not hide the joy in his voice as he regaled me with stories of how those salespeople were perpetually shut out and had no chance of taking the account from him.

Lonnie's attention to detail in getting every item delivered to the right department in the right place was tedious and slow (I now understood why he got started so much earlier than everyone else), but he believed in perfection when it came to his customers. What stood out, though, was the trust he had built with his key contacts.

Each department head received and was required to sign an invoice and detailed delivery report. Before giving them the invoice, Lonnie provided an explanation for anything that was missing, reviewed makeups from the week before, and discussed any problems. The department heads never looked at the invoices; they just signed and handed them back to Lonnie. They didn't check to see if Lonnie had made the credits he'd mentioned. They did not count the deliveries or check Lonnie. For them, Lonnie's word was gold. I'd been out with one of Lonnie's peers the day before (to establish a baseline for my ride with Lonnie) and had a totally different experience. His customers had gone through each invoice in detail, asked questions, drilled him on mistakes, and insisted on credits and write-offs. There'd been a confrontation at every stop.

Later, when I asked the purchasing manager at the plant about Lonnie, his praise was glowing. "I've been in purchasing for 20 years and I can honestly say that I've never experienced anyone like Lonnie." I asked him if he ever talked to or took bids from Lonnie's competitors. "There would be a riot around here if anyone got wind that I was shopping around. As long as Lonnie is servicing our account, we will never make a change."

Each of Lonnie's customers was different, but the response to Lonnie was the same. They were happy to see him. In fact, they looked forward to his visits because it was such a good experience. He was respected, loved, and trusted implicitly. Lonnie's success at building this rock solid foundation of trust was driven by a number of core behavior traits.

Customer First: Lonnie put the welfare and happiness of his customers before everything else. He worked hard, getting up early and staying late, to ensure his customers had a great experience. Lonnie took no shortcuts and he made it easy for his customers to do business with him. He always gave and did more than was required of him.

Attitude and Accountability: Lonnie worked in a depot that was dysfunctional and chaotic. His company and managers provided little support, and it seemed like, in many cases, they were working against him. Was Lonnie frustrated? You bet he was. Yet, I never heard him once blame this company, manager, office, or anyone or anything else for mistakes, missing products, or quality deficiencies. When there was a problem, he took responsibility and let his customer know how *he* would fix it. He took copious notes to ensure he did not forget or fail to follow through on his promises. Lonnie never used the word *they* to deflect blame for customer complaints. His attitude was clear—to my customers, I am the company.

Emotional Connections: When Lonnie was in front of customers, he was on stage. He was likable, polite, and fun to be around. He connected with his customers emotionally. He listened to them, knew their names, and asked about the important things happening in their personal lives. When Lonnie walked into a customer's building, he was on stage. His enthusiasm when working with his customers was infectious and he found ways, large and small (doughnuts and asking about a receptionist's sick mother), to create positive emotional experiences.

Spending time with Lonnie left a profound impact on me. Watching him work with his customers was humbling. Lonnie proved to me that there are no excuses for delivering poor customer experiences. I've made it my mission to hold myself and my company up to the standard he sets every day.

Going the Extra Mile

Lonnie is not just legendary with his customers; people at his company speak of him as if he were a deity. Yet, few of them really understand or even try to understand what makes Lonnie so special. They all acknowledge that his performance is extraordinary but to them, Lonnie is mystery.

If they took a moment and looked closely, they'd see that Lonnie simply goes the extra mile in everything he does for his customers. He always does more than he has to. For example, while other reps show up to their accounts and make excuses, Lonnie gets to work several hours before they do to ensure he is prepared to serve his accounts.

Most account managers and customer service reps do a good job. They come to work and work hard. They do what is expected. They earn a paycheck by keeping customers satisfied and relatively happy. For these first milers, good enough is good enough.

People like Lonnie are different. Their customers love them because every interaction is a rewarding experience. These men and women go beyond just being good. Because they give more, work harder, hustle, overcome obstacles, and do the things that others are unwilling to do, they become legendary and their customers love them.

Going the extra mile is a commitment to excellence. It is the willingness and discipline to do the right thing even when no one is watching. People who go the extra mile put their customers first. They always give more than required. Going the extra mile sets you apart from 99 percent of your competitors. It lifts you up in the eyes of your customers and builds trust.

Gary manages a book of manufacturing accounts that purchase conveyer belts, parts, and services from his company. On a recent vacation with his family, he spent an afternoon working to ensure that the installation crew was taking care of one of his customers who had ordered a new conveyer system. "I could have just let the folks in the office handle it, but my customer was nervous that the line would not be up in time for the next shift. So I remained personally involved until all of the checks and tests were completed and the line went into production. It made my customer very happy. He even said that he'd never had someone so concerned about making sure the job was done right." The next week that same customer gave Gary's company an order to replace every line in the plant on one condition—Gary had to be the account manager.

Most people would have turned their phones off and let the folks back in the office manage the installation. They would have gone to the beach and not given it another thought. After all, they were *off the clock*.

Account managers who go the extra mile are never truly off the clock when it comes to customers. For them, customers come first. Gary's customer watched his actions. He observed that Gary was committed to following through on his promises and proved that he could be trusted. That trust was rewarded with more business.

Roger Staubach once said, "There are no traffic jams on the extra mile." I'm here to tell you that when it comes to customer service, the extra mile is desolate. Trust me, you'll be there all by yourself. On the extra mile, the bar is low. Because most people give only what is required, even small things, like taking a little time from your vacation to be sure an installation goes as planned, make a massive impact on how your customers feel about *you*.

Going the extra mile is an attitude, driven by your internal belief system. It is a commitment to excellence in everything you do—even when no one is looking. By providing consistent evidence that you always give and do more than required, over time, you build a solid foundation of trust.

Customers Are Vulnerable and They Don't Trust You

When customers rely on you to deliver on promises, they are putting themselves in a vulnerable position with their money, time, and in some cases, their jobs. Your customer's reliance on you creates such vulnerability that, should you fail to perform, the impact on their business, company, or career could be extreme.

We have all experienced the emotional, and in some cases, financial pain that results from getting burned by or having our trust broken by another person. Beginning in childhood, when we first experience the pain of broken trust and into adulthood, as these experiences become cumulative, we carry skepticism and suspicion into our relationships as a means of protecting ourselves from vulnerability.

The paradox is, for the most part, we really want to trust others. Suspicion and skepticism are uncomfortable feelings. Trust feels good. Trust is stability—a state of well-being we long for. Some people give the gift of trust much more freely than others, who, for lack of better words, are perpetually living in the *show-me state*. Most people, however, given enough consistent evidence that you keep your word and do what you say you'll do, will begin to trust you.

The late Stephen R. Covey, author of *The 7 Habits of Highly Effective People,* likened building trust to making deposits in a bank account. Using this metaphor, Covey explained that you build trust by making regular deposits (consistent evidence that you are trustworthy) in another person's emotional bank account. As you make deposits, like keeping commitments and delivering on promises, the balance of trust in the account grows. When you fail to honor commitments, renege on promises, make the other person feel unimportant or unappreciated, behave in an unlikable or inconsistent way, you make withdrawals. The theory is, by making regular deposits, trust will be maintained, and there will be greater tolerance for your future indiscretions or mistakes. However, like any bank account, when you make too many withdrawals and allow your account balance to become overdrawn, there are penalties. You lose trust and place the relationship in jeopardy.

Though many factors contribute to the trust your customers have in you, the important takeaway from this metaphor is that trust is something you earn. Building and maintaining trust in business relationships means providing *consistent* evidence that you can be trusted. In Covey's view, each relationship begins with a neutral balance in the emotional bank account. I believe that customer relationships begin in the *red*. Customers have been burned so many times that until you lay a foundation of trust with consistent evidence that you are trustworthy, they will be suspicious of your motivations.

Trust is the sole foundation on which the relationships you build with your customers rest. Every action, decision, and behavior links to and directly affects trust—positively or negatively. Without trust, your customer's experience is one of uncomfortable suspicion, anxiety, anger, and ill will.

You Are Always On Stage

A trap many account managers fall into is assuming they have more trust in the emotional bank account than they really do. They falsely believe that charm, charisma, and likability are more important than showing up to meetings on time, being prepared, meeting deadlines, solving problems, being truthful or following through on promises.

As I stated earlier, most people want to find reasons to trust you. This is why your customers watch, scrutinize, and analyze your every behavior and every action. Imagine standing on a stage in an auditorium. In the audience are your clients. Your every behavior is being analyzed. You are being observed to see if your actions are congruent with your words. Perhaps you are polite to some people, but not others. Perhaps you become agitated at a minor inconvenience. Maybe you were late to a meeting and did not call in advance or didn't return an e-mail or voice mail in a timely manner. You could have missed a key piece of information that your client asked you to remember. Maybe there were typos on your last report. You told a little white lie and got caught. Took a shortcut. Covered up a mistake. Judgments are being made about how much to trust you.

In account management and customer service, you are always on stage. You must exert a tremendous amount of self-discipline to manage every behavior, promise, and action while in front of your audience. This is where the rubber meets the road. This is where emotion collides with logic. The foundation of trust is built one brick at a time based on the consistent and ongoing evidence that you are trustworthy.

Consistent Behavior

Because trusting you puts your customers in such a vulnerable position, inconsistent behavior is a huge red flag. When you are unpredictable, it is hard for people to trust you. This brings us full circle to the metaphor of business as a stage. Upon this stage, your behaviors are front and center. When you act out of character (for example, if you normally have a relaxed, professional demeanor but in a moment of irritation lose your temper), it affects your clients' trust in you.

If repeated, these instances combine to crumble any foundation of trust you've built. Inconsistent behavior can cause irreparable damage. As we are all aware, it has derailed promising careers, ruined political campaigns, and sank business deals. You control what others are allowed to observe. Think before you speak. Learn to pause and consider the consequences of rash action. With trust, you are always on stage.

Sweat the Small Stuff

When it comes to trust, especially when dealing with customers, little things make a big difference. Although there are situations in which one big lapse in judgment injures trust to such an extent that there is no going back, these events are rare. As a rule, it is the culmination of many small breaches that weaken or destroy the foundation of trust.

Things such as showing up late for meetings, not returning phone calls, disorganization, missing project deadlines, spelling and grammatical errors on written documents, being unprepared for meetings, inaccurate facts, inconsiderate behavior, failure to follow up, and constantly making excuses all seem very small. However, over time they add up and build the case that you cannot be trusted.

In today's competitive environment, hungry lions (your competitors' salespeople) are clawing at the door. For this reason, you cannot afford the luxury of a slipup. There is just too much at stake. Little things quickly turn into big things so you need to put systems and support in place to keep you organized and manage time, projects, and relationships.

Leverage Your Support Team

Imagine this: It's vacation time. Your family eagerly piles into the car. Earlier you filled the car up with gas, packed a picnic lunch, and loaded the luggage. As you pull out of the driveway, one of the kids in the backseat asks, "Where are we going?"

You shrug your shoulders and say, "Somewhere."

"Well, how will we know when we get there?" asks a small voice from the backseat.

"I'll tell you when we get there," you say emphatically. "Now be quiet and let me drive."

Sound ridiculous? It happens far too often with customers when account managers do not have a clear plan for their accounts. A strategic account plan is especially important with large accounts that are supported by a team. This ensures that everyone knows where they are going and has a map to get there.

Account managers who fail to clearly articulate the account plan to their team or company fail as advocates for their customers, because they do not effectively align internal resources to best solve customer problems. Inexplicably, they believe that everyone *should just know* what to do.

Sometimes, they hand the keys to an account to their support team and say, "Drive." Then, they are flabbergasted when their team doesn't drive in the right direction and their customer becomes upset. The account manager yells and screams at the driver for going in the wrong direction. When the support team says, "Okay, which way do you want me to go?", the account manager's only answer is, "Not this way! I don't understand why you aren't getting this!" Eventually, the support team loses faith in the account manager and disengages.

There are few lone wolves in business these days. You count on other people for support. The most successful customer service professionals and account managers have learned how to leverage their support teams to build trust with prospects and customers. They maintain ongoing strategic relationships with the people in their companies who have the resources and know how to back them up and get things done for their customers. By involving a diverse group of people who have specialization in key areas, they are able to offer more robust and relevant solutions to their customers' problems. Most importantly, because they delegate tasks to their support staff, they have more time to spend developing relationships.

When I was a national account manager, my customer base of 20-plus accounts included companies like Harley-Davidson, Chrysler, and UPS. In each of these accounts, I had multiple contacts and complex service deliverables. It was impossible to manage all of my accounts effectively without help. However, many of my peers who had similar account portfolios did just that, leaving them tired, exasperated, and scrambling every day to catch up. I saw the horror stories firsthand when the little misses here and there added up and a strategic account was lost to a competitor (there was usually a subsequent firing of an account manager).

As national account managers, we were paid for retaining *and* growing our accounts and to maximize our paychecks and keep our jobs, I needed to do both. The only way that was possible was to leverage other people. I worked hard to build and maintain relationships with people in my company who could help me. It didn't take long until I had other people doing most of the grunt work for my accounts: reports, tracking down problems, managing projects, and so on. That left me time to focus on building the relationships, looking for opportunities to grow, and creating positive emotional experiences for my contacts. And because I had a support staff at my back, it was easier to go the extra mile and build a solid foundation of trust.

Let me be clear. The support staff I used for help was available to all of my peers. I didn't manipulate the system or people. I just asked for help, treated people with respect, let go of some control, and aligned the right people to my clients and tasks.

You may believe that you have no one to help and you are working alone. You may believe that the people who are supposed to be helping you won't, or are incapable of helping you. If you think this way, you are hurting yourself and your customers. In every organization, there are people assigned to solve specific problems and get stuff done. If you don't know who these people are, ask questions and keep asking until you find out. Sometimes these people are assigned to help you on a formal basis and sometimes there is an informal system. In either case, it is *your* responsibility to build relationships with these valuable resources and work hard at those relationships.

If the phrase, *"But Jeb, you don't understand my company, my situation, my customers, my support staff,"* or some other variation of *"But Jeb"* entered your mind or crossed your lips, you will get no sympathy from me. None. I already know that your product, service, company, boss, service center, corporate HQ, support staff, billing department, warehouse, shippers, local service center, and the like are flawed. All companies have flaws with their systems and people. It is your job and responsibility to mitigate those flaws and deliver a great customer experience. You simply cannot do that alone. So, stop whining, worrying, and wishing, and get to work leveraging your support team.

Once you have your team engaged, you must provide consistent and ongoing communication and follow up. One of my favorite sayings is: "In God we trust; everyone else, we follow up on." Communication is critical because it ensures that your support team remains engaged with your customers and keeps the ball moving forward on your to-do list. Regular communication demonstrates that you care, keeps you connected to the people you need on your side, and gives you the opportunity to provide positive feedback and appreciation. This, in turn, motivates the support staff to work even harder for you. Far too many account managers fail to communicate on a regular basis and find themselves scrambling at the last moment because critical tasks were left undone or incomplete. These same people are quick to point the finger at their support staff when, in reality, they have no one to blame but themselves. Never forget that you bear the responsibility to consistently communicate and follow up—not the other way around.

I've always been appalled at customer service professionals who treat the support staff with indifference. Even worse are those who are demanding and rude—especially with last minute requests that create disruption and inconvenience to people they need to have their backs. Remember that the people on your support team are people just like you. They want to be respected, to do worthwhile work, and to feel important and appreciated. Take the time to get to know them individually. Find out what makes them tick. Understand how they are compensated, how they like to operate, and where they have the most experience. Give them the same respect you expect to receive. And, above all, be sure to thank them for the work they do.

Leveraging your support team is a powerful way to build trust and deliver legendary customer experiences. Of course, when your support staff fails to deliver on commitments, it damages the trust you've built with your clients. Therefore, you must take responsibility and accountability for their actions. This requires both planning and leadership.

You must understand, though, that leading a support team is not like managing employees. In most cases, these people don't work for you and you do not have the authority to tell them what to do. Instead, you must convince your support team to work in your customer's best interest, not because they have to, but because they want to. It is your commitment to plan and organize, the discipline to communicate and follow up effectively, and the effort to build and maintain relationships that gets and keeps the support team on your side.

Effective Time and Resource Management

Managing customer relationships is complex and demanding. In our hypercompetitive marketplace, even small slipups can quickly open the door for your competitors. If you are not organized with a plan for managing each day, those slipups will happen with greater frequency.

Time management is best defined as *getting the most out of each day by planning the most efficient use of scarce resources.* Your scarcest resource is time. My intent here is not to offend or patronize you by suggesting that you get a time management system. I know that you already have one. Likewise, I don't have the room in a book like this to teach you a time management system. What I will tell you is, there is one constant for every person—time. Time is the great equalizer. Every person (including your competitors) has exactly 24 hours each day and there are only a handful of these hours available for interacting with customers. How you use time plays an important role in how well you build trust with your customers.

My goal in this section is to create awareness for you to see what is working or not working with your current time management system. I also want you to take a second look at tools you may already be using or should be using to better manage your time and resources. The benefits of effective time and resource management are many, including: less stress and worry, lower expenses, happier customers, account growth, a higher income, and more time to spend with your family. Simply put, when you master time and resource management you are happier, healthier, and you make more money.

Effective time and resource management begins with a CEO mindset. This is an attitude and belief that you are the CEO of *You, Inc.* You must accept complete responsibility and accountability for managing your time and resources. This attitude and mindset will keep you on track and focused.

Once you take that responsibility, the next step is gaining a clear understanding of your accounts. Unfortunately, many account managers have never taken time to thoroughly analyze their customers for profitability, geographic distribution, demands and service needs, order frequency and patterns, contract requirements, growth opportunities, and so on. Instead, they work hour by hour and day to day in a reactionary mode. This often causes them to waste time with low-profit customers and low return tasks. Here is a good way to analyze your accounts:

- Rank by revenue.
- Rank by profitability.
- Rank by the time spent on each account monthly.
- Rank by growth potential.
- List accounts that are in jeopardy.
- Group accounts by contract renewal dates.
- Group accounts by geographic distribution.
- Are you spending time with the right accounts?
- Should you change how you prioritize your accounts?
- Should you change your visitation and call schedule for each account?
- Are there creative ways to manage and develop hard-to-get-to, low revenue or low profit accounts?

Account Managers who go through this process are almost always surprised by what they find. Many discover that they are spending far too much time with the wrong customers. Most are shocked that the way they rank customers based on data is much different than their initial perception. These questions and more are crucial to understanding where and with whom you will get the highest return on your time investment and the most efficient use of scarce resources.

I won't spend a great deal of time discussing tools. Time management tools are available everywhere. From the basic MS Outlook Calendar to the thousands of cutting edge apps for mobile devices, there is simply no shortage of tools available to help you manage time, tasks, and resources. My recommendation is to find the ones that work best for you and then use them in the way that works best for you. There is one tool, however, that you must have and must use consistently—the customer relationship management system or CRM.

It is highly probable that you are already using a CRM because most smart companies have one in place. If your company does not have a CRM and you are the owner, get one. There are dozens of options on the market and the cost is minimal. If your company will not invest in a CRM and you are responsible for managing accounts, get one on your own. You will more than pay for it with lower stress, a better work-life balance and a higher income.

Your CRM is the most important tool in your account management arsenal for one very important reason: It allows you to manage the details and tasks related to many different accounts and contacts without having to remember everything. Your CRM keeps you organized, your projects on track, and your relationships from getting derailed. But only if you use it!

Now, here's the deal. I can get on my soapbox and preach. I can warn you of the consequences. I can explain the benefits. But the only person who can motivate you to fully exploit your CRM is you. My philosophy is simple: Put every detail about every account and every interaction with every account and contact in your CRM. Make good clear notes. Never procrastinate. I know that it is totally a pain in the rear to stop and add detailed information into your CRM. However, if you wait until you *have time*, you will either never get the information into your system or the information will be incomplete. In account management and customer service, the little things are big things and a well-managed CRM will prevent slipups that could cost you your customers.

Don't Let Customers Find Your Problems

Jessica knocked on Henry's door. "Ready for our review?"

Henry, the buyer for a chemical manufacturing and distribution company, motioned for her to come in and sit down. Jessica is the district manager for the company providing facility services at Henry's plant.

"Henry, as you know, this is our quarterly quality service review. In this review, you have the opportunity to rate our service levels across multiple categories on a scale of 1 to 10. Before we get started though, I want to share my observations on some areas where I believe we can improve."

Henry leaned forward in his chair as Jessica turned her notes around so he could see. "Sounds good, Jessica. Thanks again for taking time to walk through the plant this morning and meet with all of our department heads."

"It was a good morning," Jessica replied. "Everyone seems to be happy with our level of service but as I walked through each department, I found a few things my people are missing. I want to review those with you as well as our action plan for improvement."

Jessica discussed the list of mostly minor issues with Henry and the plan of action for each. She also committed to dates when the issues would be fixed. Then she handed Henry her quality service review scorecard, or QSR as it was referred to in her company, and waited nervously. Henry took a minute to complete the survey and handed it back with a smile.

She looked over her scores. All 10s!

I want you to consider the exchange between Jessica and Henry for just a moment. Jessica told Henry where there were specific problems with her service. Yet, he still gave her a perfect score.

This wasn't an anomaly. When Jessica's manager sent me to ride with her, he told me that her customers loved her. Jessica's average QSR score was 9.7. The average score of all of the district managers in her company was 6.8. When I interviewed Jessica's customers privately, they told me:

"Jessica is always there when we need her."

"The most responsive vendor we work with."

"No matter what happens, she gets it fixed without a hassle."

"I trust her."

"I hope her company knows what an asset she is. If we didn't have her on our account, I don't know what we would do."

"Jessica is proactive. She is always one step ahead of me."

"She is special. I don't work with anyone else like her."

As I followed her though the day, she consistently pointed out to her customers where she and her company had room for improvement—always followed up by a plan of action and a follow-up date. When I asked her why she would blatantly point out service and quality deficiencies, her response was direct and simple. "Never let customers find your mistakes. That's when they get upset."

Most account managers and their leaders hide from quality and service problems, hoping that somehow they will go away or that they can fix the issue before their customer ever finds out. Sometimes this works. Sometimes it does not. When it does not, and your customer discovers your mistake, they remember it as a poor experience. On the other hand, if you cover up your mistake, and they never find you out, you miss an extraordinary opportunity to build a foundation of trust and frame your customer's experience in a unique way.

The very best account managers share Jessica's philosophy: *Never let customers find your mistakes.* Of course, they are realistic enough to understand that no matter what they do, in time, their customer will point out a problem. The fact is you and your company are going to make mistakes. You are going to screw up—in big and small ways. The difference though is when you make this your philosophy (*Never let customers find your mistakes)* you become more proactive. You become focused on constantly looking for opportunities to improve. Because it is your mission to discover mistakes and issues before your customer points them out to you, small problems rarely become big problems. So instead of wasting time constantly cleaning up and reacting to messes, you are able to spend more time developing enduring relationships and uncovering opportunities to grow your accounts.

The most important by-product of *never letting your customers find your mistakes* is that it builds an incredibly strong foundation of trust and delivers an extraordinary customer experience.

When you point out where you have an opportunity to improve or tell your customer you screwed up and what you are going to do to fix it, you do the unexpected. Instead of the uncomfortable and often emotionally painful confrontations customers are used to experiencing, there is a refreshing sense of relief. You rise above virtually every other vendor they deal with and gain instant and lasting credibility.

This past summer, a programming mistake created a situation where the advertising traffic one of our customers was paying for was being delivered to broken links. We discovered the issue about a week after it happened and quickly fixed it. It was a small blip and because our customer managed many campaigns across hundreds of websites, they never noticed and it was unlikely that they would have ever known had we not told them. The account manager assigned to their account immediately let them know what had happened and offered a make-good solution. A few days later, we received this note from our contact:

> "We appreciate your proactive, professional, honest, and genuine approach. We appreciate your partnership and value the great service you provide. No worries—it happens to the best of us and we know you guys handled this like rock stars."

Where we had been just one of many advertising vendors (just another website) now we were *rock stars*—and an important partner. We stood out. We had credibility. We went the extra mile. We could be trusted. Over the next two months, they doubled their ad spend with us. Today our partnership is stronger than ever and still growing.

Admit When You Are Wrong and Apologize

It is in our nature as humans to save face. Few of us take any pleasure in admitting when we are wrong. It is especially difficult to apologize in embarrassing situations or when your customer is angry and confrontational. Customers, however, don't really care about human nature or your pride. They become irritated and distrustful when dealing with customer service professionals who are defensive and seem unwilling to accept any responsibility for mistakes. You have dealt with these people in your own life and you know how it feels.

The fact is, sooner or later you are going to personally screw up and let your customer down. Things like failing to keep a commitment, having to go back on a promise, or missing a meeting or scheduled call shouldn't happen, but they sometimes do. You are human.

When you make a mistake, face up to the situation as quickly as possible and apologize. Apologies and admitting where you have been wrong provide your customer with the opportunity to observe your character. Sincere apologies are accepted and appreciated, and they demonstrate your integrity (provided you are not apologizing for the same mistake again and again). Sincere apologies also quickly diffuse confrontation and tension in customer service situations. The key is humility (putting your pride aside), timeliness, and sincerity. A little humor or creativity, especially in an embarrassing situation, can also go a long way.

To the Customer, *You* Are the Company

Of course, it is one thing to apologize when the mistake is your own. It is an entirely different thing when the issue was caused by someone else. The reality is, as an account manager or customer service rep, there are so many things out of your direct control that impact your customer. You'll spend much more of your time apologizing for these things than for your own failures.

Here is a brutal fact that you must understand: The quickest way to lose your customer's trust and ultimately your customer is to blame **THEY**.

I'm sorry, there isn't much I can do about it. **THEY** made the
rule that way.
THEY told me I couldn't.
THEY screwed up the delivery.
THEY didn't get it done in time.
I don't understand why **THEY** keep doing that.

Blaming *they* has an endless array of variations including
blaming the computers, system, warehouse, production facility,
office, and the list goes on.

The net result is each time you push blame off on someone or
something else, you weaken the foundation of trust you have with
your customer and diminish the respect they have for you. You see,
your customer does not care about *they*. Your customer will never
love *they*. To your customer, *you* are the company. *You* are the warehouse, office, computer, shippers, production facility, engineers, or
service crew.

Your customer trusts *you* to solve their problems. When you
blame *they*, *you* become smaller. When you abdicate responsibility
and accountability for your customer's problems, concerns, happiness, and experience by deflecting blame on others, you are no
longer a worthwhile partner and you open the door to your competitors to steal your accounts.

Look, I know it is hard to suck it up when you are getting
your butt kicked by a customer for something that was out of your
control. It stinks and you'll naturally default to defense. Don't do it.
Instead, take a breath, pause, and say, "I'm sorry." Then take responsibility and get to work solving the problem.

Here is the bottom line: No matter how good your product
or service; no matter how well known your company brand; no
matter how likable you are, how hard you work, how many problems you solve, or how many nice things you do, you absolutely,
positively, cannot deliver a legendary customer experience without
a solid foundation of trust between you and your customer.

8

Create Positive Emotional Experiences

My phone rang early on a Saturday morning. I rolled over in bed and squinted at the screen. *Who in the world is calling me this early?* "Hello?"

"Hey Jeb, what are you doing?" The chipper voice on the other line was bright and full of energy. *Ugh.*

I peeked at the clock. *Six in the morning!* I'd pulled in after midnight from the airport after a long week on the road. My fantasy of sleeping in had just been dashed. "I was sleeping, Jodi, what's up?"

"Oh I'm sorry, I didn't realize how early it was. Look, I just sent over an e-mail. I need y'all to overnight 20 *People Buy You* books to me. I've got a big project meeting with a customer next week and I want to do something nice for their people. But here's the thing. I need you to personalize each of them. There are instructions for how I want you to sign each book in the e-mail." Then her voice softened. "You sound tired. You haven't been working too hard, have you?"

I got up. We chatted about clients and traveling and kids. Then I sat down in my office and signed each book. Jodi had provided a special personalized message for each person on her list. Classic Jodi.

Jodi is one of the best relationship builders I've ever met. She takes time to get to know people and understands what is important to them. She has developed the skill to hear people and hone in on what is most important to them. As vice president of business development for Bluewave, a company that provides services to large telecom companies, she works tirelessly to develop and maintain relationships from top to bottom with the decision makers and key influencers at those companies.

"There are only a handful of big telecom companies and the competition for their attention and the millions of dollars of contracts they hand out is intense," Jodi explains. "It's not just about doing a high-quality job or delivering great service. That is a base expectation that most of my competitors can live up to. I've got to make sure they are always thinking about Bluewave. I've got to be sure that they trust us, like us, and that I am the first person they call when a new contract is about to go out."

Jodi works relentlessly to anchor her customer relationships. She spends time getting to know her clients personally and works to create positive emotional experiences for them, big and small. Whether she is entertaining at the Kentucky Derby, playing golf at Doral, hosting clients at Mardi Gras, remembering to send a simple birthday card, or getting an author to personalize a book for her contacts, she builds strong emotional connections with her clients through sincere, personalized gestures.

Emotion Trumps Logic

Sadly, many account managers believe that if customers are happy with the product or service, they will keep buying for that reason. They falsely believe that logic alone drives the decisions customers make about who to do business with. This is why account managers have the tendency to ignore customers who are not complaining. However, you ignore customers at your peril. In Jodi's industry the stakes are high. Losing a large contract could mean layoffs at her company that impact dozens of employees. Losing a customer puts the entire company at risk. This is why top account managers never rely on the product or service to anchor their relationships.

Have you ever had a customer quit you out of the blue, for no apparent reason? The conversation often goes like this:

"Hi Bill, we've decided to go in a different direction. We're going to give one of your competitors a try."

"I don't understand, John, I thought you were happy with the service we've been providing. You even said so on your last customer satisfaction survey. Why would you take a chance on those guys when we have proven that we deliver?"

"Bill, we just think it is time to try something new."

The brutal fact is, as soon as you forgot to appreciate your client, someone else is starting to show him appreciation. That someone else is most often Mr. Schmooze: a smartly dressed, glad handing sales pro from your competitor, who takes the time to make your customer feel important and appreciated in your absence.

In the experience economy, if you lose the emotional connection with your customer, you are toast. The reality is, no matter how good your product or service, there are 10 salespeople knocking on your customer's door selling the same or similar products or services. In the hypercompetitive global economy, products and services can and will be duplicated quickly. The one thing they cannot duplicate, though, is *you*. This is why it is critical to anchor customers to *you* on an emotional level. If you don't keep your customers thinking about *you*, sooner or later someone else will come along and win them over.

Anchoring Relationships

At sea, an anchor creates a bond between the ocean floor and a vessel. A big metal hook on the ocean floor is attached to the ship by a chain. That bond holds the vessel stationary and safe.

It is important to note that anchors cannot be dropped to the ocean floor and forgotten. Captains must relentlessly monitor their anchors to ensure they are holding fast and not dragging. Constant changes in wind, currents, tide, and the sea floor all conspire to unhook the anchor and leave the ship adrift—a disaster waiting to happen.

Customer relationships must be anchored, too. In relationships, an anchor creates an emotional bond between you and another person. This aids in holding the relationship together and safe. The emotional anchors that hold your relationships firm require the same vigilance as an anchor at sea. Relationships that are ignored eventually go adrift.

There is a saying: *Always leave them wanting more.* This saying is applied most often to performers who work on the stage—actors, speakers, musicians, and comedians. Leaving them wanting more is part of the audience's emotional experience. This line is just as appropriate to account managers and customer service professionals for whom business is the stage. It is essential that you never forget that you are always on stage. If you want to retain your clients, grow your accounts, and deliver legendary customers experiences, you must strive in every interaction to leave your customers wanting more of *you.*

Remember Lonnie from the previous chapter? What if your customers really looked forward to your calls or visits? What if your customers told your competitors that they would never leave you? What if they were more forgiving of inevitable shortfalls and service issues? What if they renewed contracts with little negotiation? What if they handed you new business without bidding it out? Calls and meetings would be very different. Just think how this would neutralize the efforts of your competitors to steal your clients and make your job easier. All of this is possible and *more* when you create *positive emotional experiences.* Creating positive emotional experiences anchors you to your customers, building stronger emotional connections and greater trust.

The Law of Reciprocity

The power that comes from creating positive emotional experiences for your customers is expressed in the Law of Reciprocity. When you act in kind ways or give to others, they naturally feel obligated to give something back to you.

In business relationships, what is given back may be in the direct form of additional business, renewed contracts, or good scores on satisfaction surveys. The more powerful obligation that customers give in return for positive emotional experiences is trust and loyalty to *you*. Where a direct payback may be a one-time event, loyalty is ongoing. You gain loyalty over the long term as positive emotional experiences add up and your clients begin to trust that you really care about them. Loyalty locks your competitors out. Loyalty forgives mistakes. Loyalty generates referrals. Loyalty gives you inside information, moves your invoices to the top of the accounts-payable file, gets you past gatekeepers, lends you a hand, and whispers in someone's ear. Loyalty goes to battle for you when the chips are down.

In his classic book, *Ultimate Success*, Frank Beaudine writes that the Law of Reciprocity is one of the great truths of life, because the more we give, the more we receive. Robert B. Cialdini, author of *The Psychology of Persuasion*, goes a step further, saying, "One of the most potent of the weapons of influence around us is the [law] for reciprocation. The [law] says that we should try to repay, in kind, what another person has provided us." In layman's terms, the Law of Reciprocity simply explains that when someone gives you something, you feel an obligation to give value back.

Notice, however, even though the Law of Reciprocity says that when you give to others they will *feel an obligation* to give back, it does not say they *will* give back. Some customers may never return your goodwill. This is why the deliberate pursuit of reciprocity, in other words approaching reciprocity as a quid pro quo transaction—I give value to you, therefore, you give equal or greater value back—does not work. Doing so will leave you jaded and frustrated because these expectations will only turn into resentment.

Creating positive emotional experiences for customers is most powerful when you sincerely want to give them joy with no expectation for anything in return. This requires faith that when you give with sincerity and for the right reasons, the universe has an amazing way of evening things out and paying you back many times over—sometimes directly and sometimes indirectly. (For inspiration on giving with no expectations of receiving anything back, visit www.helpothers.org.)

Unfortunately, far too many account managers choose to ignore this universal truth and instead live by the motto, *Me first*. They argue that they've "tried to give to customers, but it doesn't work because everyone is just out to take advantage of them." They have no faith in the Law of Reciprocity and they are quick to regale you with stories of how customers have screwed them over.

When dealing with customers, this *me-first* attitude has a significant and negative impact on your relationships. Account managers who view their customers with cynicism and distrust or as a means to an end (their paycheck) are on a path that leads only to failure.

Pay Attention to Self-Disclosures (Listen Deeply)

What you experience is what you remember. The more emotional the experience, the deeper it is branded into your memory. When you consistently create positive experiences for your clients, you add to that memory and deepen their emotional connection with you.

Positive emotional experiences create stronger relationship anchors when your actions are thoughtful and personal. Knowing the right thing to do in your unique situation only requires that you listen and be creative. For example, an account manager sent a simple card to her client, explaining: "His wife had just had a baby. I was talking to him one day and he seemed stressed and tired. So I got a funny card and wrote, 'Take some time for yourself. New dads need rest, too.' It really touched him. It has been two years and he still thanks me for thinking about him."

The secret to uncovering opportunities to create personalized, thoughtful, and positive emotional experiences that make others feel appreciated and valued is listening deeply for self-disclosure. You'll recall that when you listen, others feel more connected to you. The more connected they feel, the more they will reveal about themselves. Focusing all your attention on the person in front of you and listening deeply with your eyes, ears, and heart will lead you to the areas that are of emotional importance to them. Focus your attention here, and you quickly find opportunities to create positive experiences that have deep emotional significance. The key is awareness. This requires you to overcome your natural self-centered tendencies.

Each day you will be presented with opportunities to create positive emotional experiences for your customers. It will be difficult to leverage these opportunities without a system for follow up. Your system should be designed to help you stay on track and remember birthdays, anniversaries, and special events. It should have processes that make it easy for you to do things like send handwritten notes. It should also remind you to follow through on random events like finding and sending a book you think your client will like. You should also have a system for planning larger events to ensure the important details that help personalize the event are not forgotten.

This is why managing your CRM becomes important—in fact, it is your most important relationship tool. Take copious notes when you are with your clients and record everything in your CRM program. Become systematic and self-disciplined in collecting and recording data that supports your efforts to create unique, personalized, and positive emotional experiences.

If you are fortunate enough to have an assistant or support person, have them set up a system to manage client touches. Then delegate as much as possible. An assistant can perform miracles when it comes to creating positive emotional experiences, while allowing you to remain focused on other high-value activities. If you do not have a company-provided assistant, consider hiring a virtual assistant. Virtual assistants work by the hour, are relatively inexpensive, and will take care of many of the little things that make a big difference over time.

Little Things Are Big Things

One executive I interviewed for this book suggested that I collect stories on the most extraordinary, out of the park, over the top things people have done to delight customers. These, of course, are the legends and lore that get written about in so many business articles and books about customer service. Companies and employees from Nordstrom, The Ritz Carlton, and Southwest Airlines tend to dominate these stories. The reason these over the top acts of kindness are written about and become legendary is because they connect with us on an emotional level. However, if we are to be honest, the opportunities to get over the top are rare, often expensive, and though they sound good in a book or article, not practical in the day-to-day world of business.

Now, I am not saying that you should not take the opportunity to do something truly epic when the opportunity arises. I once made arrangements to have one of my customers spend time practicing with the pit crew of his favorite NASCAR driver and then later meet that driver at Bristol. It was his ultimate fantasy and in his words, "The greatest thing anyone has ever done for me." It was a once in a lifetime experience and was only made possible through a couple of fortuitous connections.

A vice president for a private bank explained how her company flies clients along with their private banker in and out of Augusta for the Masters on a corporate jet. Clients get club house passes, play golf at top courses, and spend the night in a local mansion. "For many of these clients, we make their lifelong dream of attending the Masters finally come true."

What is important to understand, however, is if you want to touch your customers and anchor them to you emotionally, the opportunities will be there day in and day out and you won't need to break the budget to create positive emotional experiences.

Brandy noticed that her customer was an advocate for the Susan G. Komen Breast Cancer Foundation. "She was always involved with fundraising activities. This was her passion. So, one day at lunch I asked her why she spent so much time working with the charity. She explained that her sister and mother had both died from breast cancer and that she was dedicated to giving whatever she could to finding a cure. Her story touched me so much that I volunteered to work with her on a walk for the cure event. I took my daughters along, too. We had an opportunity to get to know each other in a different setting and connect in a special way.

Lori manages accounts in the dental industry. "A couple of years ago, while visiting one of my top dentists he shared that he was trying to find a Wii for his son for Christmas, but was having no luck. Two weeks later I came across a Wii and bought it. I called the office and let the doctor know I had found him one. He could not believe that with over 500 accounts, I remembered his 'problem.' I had it delivered to his office the next day. To this day, he introduces me to any new doctors or staff as the 'best rep ever.' It makes me feel great that I was able to help him and that he was impressed that I 'heard' what he needed and solved the problem for him, even though it was not dentally related."

Leanne Hoagland-Smith, author of *be the Red Jacket in a Sea of Grey Suits*, says, "Sometimes the most over the top actions are just simple ones of gratitude. Sending a congratulations card for achieving a significant goal to creating a tool for improved productivity or communications when hearing of a need reflects your gratitude for your clients being clients and more importantly, being people who have wants and needs."

Tim, who owns a consulting business, sends a letter to his contact's boss detailing their level of work or professionalism. "The letter is usually two pages detailing specific milestones and events where my contact has demonstrated quality work. Each time I do this it creates an instant and powerful connection." The trick, he says, is *not* to do it for self-serving purposes. "You must be honest and sincere." Tim's example proves that as long as your gesture is sincere and personal, when creating positive emotional experiences for customers, little things are big things:

- A phone call to congratulate an accomplishment
- A handwritten thank-you note
- Birthday cards
- Anniversary cards
- A framed newspaper or magazine clipping of a client receiving an award or article about her company
- An unexpected gift commemorating a special occasion
- Concert tickets along with special VIP access
- Tickets to a major event like the Masters, World Series, or Daytona 500
- Unique meals
- Getting a client access to drive a race car
- Helping a client's child get an interview, a golf lesson, or a meeting with an important person
- Sending flowers to a funeral
- Giving an autographed picture of a celebrity
- A round of golf at an exclusive club

The opportunities to create positive emotional experiences are endless. For example, technology and the Internet have made gathering information about others as simple as a few keystrokes on Google, Facebook, or LinkedIn. An easy way to prepare for meetings with customers is to do a quick online search to look for accomplishments or events that they will be proud to talk about. When you ask a customer about personal achievements or important events in their lives, you give the opportunity to talk about something that makes them feel important. You demonstrate that you care and are paying attention to them, which makes them feel appreciated and valued.

All people have a deep need for approval of their actions and accomplishments. This is one of our most basic and powerful human desires; one which is ongoing and never completely satisfied. Bestselling author and speaker Brian Tracy says,

"People who continually seek opportunities to express approval are welcome wherever they go."

Small acts of kindness have a lasting impact and allow you to tap into the true power of the law of reciprocity. Certainly, big experiences like taking a client who loves NASCAR into the pit to meet his favorite driver can cost thousands of dollars and create lasting memories. However, being thoughtful doesn't have to cost much of anything. In many cases, small gestures carry far more meaning than big ones. Remembering a client's birthday or important family event, sending a handwritten thank-you note, or leaving a congratulatory voice mail are all easy and essentially free ways to create positive emotional experiences. It is all about being creative, making it personal, and having the self-discipline to follow through.

Take Action

Good intentions mean nothing. Creating positive emotional experiences requires taking action to do something kind for another person for the sole purpose of making them feel good. The discipline to take action and to follow through is essential. Many people have the intention to create positive emotional experiences. Few have the discipline to follow through.

Robert Louis Stevenson said, "Don't judge each day by the harvest you reap but by the seeds you plant." The Law of Reciprocity says you have to give in advance. You only get back after you give. If you don't take action, you get nothing. I wish it were different. I wish that we could blink our eyes, wave a wand, or wiggle our noses and all the hard work of creating positive emotional experiences would be done. As we all know, it doesn't work that way.

9 | Make Breaking Up Hard to Do

Nick was at his wits' end. *What else could he do?* Three months earlier, his customer Derek called to express his dissatisfaction and had asked to get out of the contract he'd signed. Nick listened to his complaints and convinced Derek to give him 90 days to get them fixed. They had even agreed on a set of metrics that, if met, would mean Derek would continue the contract.

Nick got his support team together and went to work. They gave it everything. "As hard as we ever worked to save an account," Nick said later. "We went way beyond what we had to do and I met with Derek every week to review the results. We were measuring everything, but despite the number I was showing him at each meeting, he'd say we were still failing."

Nick's team hunkered down and worked even harder, but after 60 days Nick realized he was getting nowhere. "The more the facts supported that we were delivering on our promise, the harder he pushed back. Frankly, he started acting like real jerk. He wasn't even listening. I realized that he never had any intention to living up to his commitment. It made me angry that we'd put that much effort into saving the account and he treated us like this. I resisted the desire to call Derek up and tell him exactly what I thought of him."

Nick did call Derek but instead of telling him off, he told Derek that he would let him out of his contract early. Derek thanked him and that was that until Nick's phone rang eight months later. "It was Derek. He wanted to talk about signing a new contract. The company he'd left us for had failed to live up to their big promises. He had saved money but was not getting good service. He's been one of my best customers for the last three years."

A bias toward account management and customer retention is the hallmark of the most profitable businesses. To succeed at building highly profitable long-term revenue streams, businesses and every employee within those businesses must become laser focused on preserving their current customer base.

Yet no matter how good your systems and processes, product quality, service delivery, and relationships, you and your company are going to piss off customers and lose others. You simply cannot be all things to all people and you will never make everyone happy all of the time. How you deal with upset customers has a real impact on their experience with you. In this short, final chapter we address dealing with pissed off customers and retaining customers in our hypercompetitive economy.

Dealing with Pissed Off Customers

Customers get mad. They get mad for lots of reasons. There will be situations where the customer is pissed off and totally wrong. There will be many more times when they are upset for a good reason. The one thing you can be sure of is when they get mad they are going to call you and there is a good chance that call will not be pleasant. What is important to understand is, regardless of why they are mad, how you handle the situation is very much part of your customer's overall experience with you. There are three important rules for dealing with upset customers:

> **Rule #1: Don't piss them off in the first place.** You might be thinking: Duh! Thanks for the blinding flash of the obvious. Of course, I know that I need to keep my customers happy.

Let me explain. When customers call to complain—even when they are unhappy—it doesn't mean they are pissed off. It just means they need help. There is a big difference between a customer who is having problems and not happy and one who is pissed off. In other words, in most instances, people don't get angry just because there is an issue with your product or service. Few customers expect you to be perfect.

The top seven things that push customers over the edge into anger or worse, into yelling, screaming, and threatening tantrums are:

1. Can't get through to you or anyone else when they need help.
2. No call back or return e-mail.
3. Failure to respond to issues quickly.
4. Broken promises.
5. Failure to keep deadlines (you are not dependable)—especially when your failure impacts their customers.
6. Same issue keeps happening again and again.
7. Instead of listening and gaining a full understanding of their situation, your first move is to prove them wrong.

Do you see the common thread here? These are all things that you can control and have little to do with your product or service. The fact is you will remove 99 percent of the reasons customers get pissed off by being accessible, providing a quick response, and being dependable (the top five). You will also notice that these are the same reasons you get pissed off when dealing with people and companies.

What is critically important to understand is when customers consistently experience you as inaccessible, someone who fails to respond quickly, and not dependable, it erodes any trust you have established. You will recall that trust is the foundation on which all relationships are built. Without trust, you will not have customers for long.

Rule #2: Don't make it worse. Another blinding flash of the obvious, though unheeded by far too many customer service professionals. Once a customer is annoyed, angry, or livid the last thing you want to do is make it worse. Start with the seven points from rule one. If one of these has contributed to pissing off your customer, make sure you don't repeat it and further injure the relationship. You also want to avoid communication mistakes that have a tendency to make things worse, such as these:

- Telling the customer to calm down or that you cannot help them until they calm down.
- Talking down to them or using a condescending tone of voice.

- Telling them that you don't like their tone of voice or "the way you are speaking to me."
- Being or sounding defensive.
- Telling them that you cannot help them: "I'm sorry sir but there is nothing I can do about that." or "That's the policy; there's nothing I can do about that."
- Blaming someone or something else.

Again, I challenge you to think about your own experiences when you've been pissed off. How did it make you feel when the customer service rep was condescending or defensive?

It is not easy when someone is yelling at you and using a tough and direct tone. It feels like they are attacking you. Your natural tendency is to defend yourself or attack back. That is why customer service professionals and account managers make the mistake of becoming defensive and arguing with their customers in an effort to defend themselves or say things like, "I'm not going to listen to you as long as you are talking to me like this." Attempts to use logic to reason with angry customers is also dead-end because to your customer, it comes off as condescending.

Any attempt to push back on a livid customer with reasoning, argument, or defensiveness is useless. It just makes it worse. The reason is simple. Emotion always trumps logic. Always. When your customer is in a high state of negative emotion, they are looking for a fight. The only thing that will diffuse the situation is to instantly fix the issue (which is rarely possible) or give them room to calm down so you have an opportunity to solve the problem and rebuild trust.

> **Rule #3: Shut up and listen.** Let them rant. Allow them to get it off of their chest. Give them the opportunity to explain. Just listen until they calm down.

My temper flared as I dialed the phone. There was no way around it; I was pissed and I was going to give these guys a piece of my mind. The lifeline for my company is our digital phone line and because we have a remote workforce, it must work perfectly all of the time. Half of our account managers were having problems getting calls. Our people were calling the help desk line but the problems persisted. The issue dropped in my lap after one of our larger customers chewed me out because we were not answering our phones.

When I contacted my account manager, Felecia, I let her have it. I was over the top but serious about my intention to move our phone service to her competitor. Poor Felecia felt the full brunt of my frustration. It was unbecoming but I'd gotten so emotional over the situation that I just lost control of my mouth. Fifteen minutes later, though, I was apologizing profusely and telling Felecia over and over again how lucky we were to have her as an account manager and pledging to never take my business elsewhere.

How did Felecia turn the situation around? Simple. She shut up and listened. Her first move was to just let me rant. She didn't interrupt. She didn't say, "Whoa there, Daddy—nobody talks to me like that!" She didn't make it worse. Instead she gave me room to get what I had to say off of my chest. I wore my own self out. Then, with a calm, kind, empathetic voice she said, "I am so sorry that your customer was upset with you. I know that put you in an uncomfortable position. I apologize that we played a role in that. May I ask you a couple of questions?"

Whoosh. All of the air went out of my sails. Deep down, I wanted a fight. But she took that away. She did not fight back—she agreed with me and she made it clear that she was going to help me. She asked me a series of questions, did some troubleshooting, and together we got to the root of the issue: We had expanded our workforce beyond the limits of our original license. My people were calling to get help setting up their systems but the system didn't work because I hadn't purchased enough lines. It was my fault.

Felecia scored major points when we came to that conclusion. Instead of throwing it back in my face—remember, I had been very ugly to her and she certainly had the right to do so—she told me not to worry and that it happens all of the time. She said it is hard to keep up with everything when you are running a growing business. She was standing in my shoes and I was putty in her hands. Felecia gave me the first month on the new licenses for free because, she said, "I should have called you to discuss your needs earlier."

One important point to remember, over the course of your career, is that *customers never complain about people who listen.* I wrote a letter to Felecia's manager explaining why she was an asset to his organization.

Listening is the key to dealing with pissed off customers because (see Rule #1) most of the time they are pissed off because no one listened to them in the first place. Remember that listening allows you to quickly build emotional connections with other people because it makes them feel important and appreciated—it gives your customer a positive emotional experience. This is why listening is so powerful when dealing with angry customers. The positive emotions they feel when you make them feel appreciated and important, trump the negative emotions they felt when they confronted you in the first place.

Listening brings your customer's emotional wall down, making them more receptive to problem solving and potential solutions. The key to breaking through this wall is starting with questions that are easy for your customer to answer and further demonstrate that you are listening. Then give them your complete attention. This is most critical. When people get your undivided attention, it makes them feel good. This reinforces answering your questions with a positive reward (a behavior that receives a positive reward tends to repeat itself), which causes your customer to want to answer more of your questions, further pulling the wall down.

The more closely you pay attention to your customer and become genuinely interested in what they are saying, the more valuable and important they will feel. The better they feel, the more they will want to talk. The more they talk, the more connected they will feel to you. As you connect, the wall will continue to come down until you gain the right to ask the deeper, more strategic questions that will eventually help you uncover and solve their problems.

Be Responsive

Over my 25 years in business, I've learned that customers value responsiveness as much as anything. Though buyers are willing to forgive mistakes, they will harshly punish companies and their representatives who fail to respond to issues quickly and divisively. Keep in mind that in our tech driven, always-on, 24/7 landscape, many customers expect and insist on instant response. This puts massive pressure on customer service professionals. Yet, it is reality and the new normal in customer relationships. Responsive account managers are loved and trusted by their customers because they:

- Stand out among the mediocre companies and reps who don't take service seriously.
- Are perceived to be more dependable.
- Solve problems that reduce disruption to their customers' businesses, saving them time and money.

Responsiveness = better customer experience. It is a tangible demonstration of your commitment to excellence and it has a huge impact on decision making both consciously and subconsciously with buyers. With buyers under increasing pressure to cut costs, every expense is being scrutinized. Even small failures in service or quality can get you thrown out. However, buyers are much more likely to work with you when you are legendary for responsiveness. You must be vigilant and fanatical about following up on every customer issue. This includes leaving nothing to chance with your own support team. Be easily accessible, respond quickly, follow through, and follow up. This must be your daily mantra.

Protect Your Turf

Devin was devastated as he reluctantly called his boss with the news that he'd lost a top 10 account. He knew that with this loss, his job was surely on the line. Earlier that day his contact called to let him know that they were not going to renew their contract and were going with one of Devin's competitors. The competitor had promised significant service improvements and savings and the buyer was convinced that making the switch was the right thing to do. Devin asked for a meeting to offer a counter proposal. The buyer refused. Then Devin begged, "Please give me a chance to show you what we can do. We've been serving your account for 10 years and if I had just known that this is what you wanted, we could have provided it for you. We've always given you great service, haven't we?" The buyer was unmoved. The decision had been made. It was over.

This same scenario plays out again and again across the business landscape. It is just part of the reality of business. Account managers are tasked with retaining customers against an onslaught of salespeople that relentlessly pound on the door. When account managers fail to proactively manage their customer relationships, those salespeople slip through the cracks and encourage buyers to consider their options. Aggressive salespeople never miss an opportunity to topple embedded, long-term relationships. The battle never ends and vigilance is the key to protecting your turf. Losing your customer base not only puts your job and income at risk, but the impact on your company can be catastrophic in this environment. Customers are essential to the survival of the organization.

As an account manager, you must take consistent daily action to protect your turf. You must take nothing for granted. Every customer and every relationship is at risk. Hoping for the best is a losing strategy. You must take systematic action to shore up and strengthen your relationships and reinforce the value of your product or service. You must respond swiftly to any real or perceived service issue no matter how small. And you must get proactive in meeting with your customers to learn about their business issues, uncover problems, and proactively suggest ways to solve those problems.

One of the hardest things to do is keep your fingers on the pulse of your customer base. It is made even harder by the fast pace of twenty-first century business and the fact that you likely have more customers that you feel you can handle. Strong, trusting relationships are the key. Devin was unaware that he was in trouble until it was too late. However, had he been managing the relationship, it is highly likely that he would have been given a heads up that would have allowed him a chance to save the business.

The key to protecting your turf is a systematic approach to account management. The first step is to block time on your schedule to create a plan. Take this time to analyze your customer base. Start with ranking and segmenting your customers based on revenue and profit contribution. Once you know where your customers rank in order of contribution to your business, take a close look at how often and in what ways you are connecting with them. How often are you contacting them through phone, e-mail, regular mail, or face-to-face interactions? What are the objectives of those interactions? Are some customers getting lots of contact while others are getting none? And where do these customers rank on your list?

Take an honest approach. Make an effort to view your account management activity through your customer's eyes. Would your relationship-building efforts make you want to buy more from your company? Would you feel like your company really cared about you as a customer? Do you think that you really understand your business problems and situations? If not, what needs to change?

Based on your analysis, develop a more systematic approach to contacting and building relationships with your customers. Decide on the frequency, objective, and methods for staying connected.

You may be constrained by budget cuts and travel restrictions so be prepared to get creative. Then execute your plan. Staying connected will help put your finger squarely on the pulse of your highest value customers while they're still customers. A book that I highly recommend reading is *The New Successful Large Account Management* by Robert B. Miller and Stephen E. Heiman. You will find a wealth of tactics and strategies for managing accounts. Getting ahead of the curve and investing in whatever it takes to retain your current customer base is like investing in an annuity that will pay back a return on that investment for years to come.

Dealing with the Pressure to Reduce Costs

Some threats are especially difficult to deal with, though, because they put you and your company in a Catch-22. When buyers pressure you for price and cost reductions, you are often pushed into a corner. The reality is, your customers are constantly looking for any and every way to cut costs. Sometimes this is just routine. In many cases, executives issue blanket orders to buyers and purchasing departments to reduce expenses by some arbitrary number like 20 percent. Sometimes department budgets are slashed. In other cases, competitors offer low-ball proposals that you are asked to match. At times, these requests are not founded in logic and are no more than fishing expeditions. Sometimes they are a serious threat.

When the cost reduction call comes in, some account managers play a game of avoidance while others panic. Their plans, bonuses, and careers pass before their eyes. Other account managers go on the defensive. Both losing strategies. Top account executives put aside panic and assume the role of a calm, logical, trusted advisor. They attempt to view the situation from their customer's perspective. What are their motivations? What is their ultimate objective? How can they create a win for their customer? How is this impacting the buyer personally? Answering these questions puts them in a position to respond with real solutions that connect with their customer's logical and emotional needs.

I am a visual person so I like to create ways to show how total program costs impact my customers. I believe that my job is to educate my customer on the difference in the *price* of our products and the total *cost* of the program. You must quantify and show these differences to your customer so you can justify the prices you are charging. You must demonstrate that while your price per product may seem slightly higher than your competitor, the *total cost* of the program (the value you bring to the account) is less, making your products and services a higher value. Start first with listing the unique benefits of your products and services for your customer. What solutions do you provide, and what financial impact does that make? Make sure not to miss the impact of soft costs that might not otherwise be taken into consideration. For example, if you provide an easy to use, closed loop customer service process, this may save your customer time when they have a problem or a question. Time is money and should be considered in the total cost equation.

Next, gather testimonials from the users of your product or service within the account. It is always amazing to see how disconnected top-level buyers are from what is happening in the real world. Be sure to use internal coaches to back up your message to the buyer. Likewise, use surveys, customer service logs, documented process improvements, sustainability, and waste reduction to demonstrate and reinforce your great track record.

Once you have completed this process with your buyer, it is rare that you won't find them moving into your court. Because of that, the conversation about reducing costs changes from adversarial to consultative. Perhaps there is nothing you can do to reduce costs and in that case, the buyer will often move on to easier pickings with other vendors. However, in many cases you can offer solutions that include process improvement, alternative products, inventory management efficiencies, waste reduction, or other opportunities to reduce overall costs without impacting price.

Most account managers are surprised at how easy this is and how receptive buyers are to their suggestions. The key is understanding their objective and developing solutions that are a win for you and your customer.

Are All Customers Good Customers?

I had a conversation recently with a friend of mine who owns a logistics company. Don told me about a particular customer that had he and his staff jumping through hoops. He was frustrated that this customer was beating him up on every aspect of his service, complaining about price and negotiating his profits down to the bone. He explained that the customer was so hard on his employees that people avoided taking their calls. The problem was that the customer represented a lot of revenue and he was concerned that if he pushed back too hard, he might lose the account. I asked him a simple question: Are all customers good customers?

The answer to this question is a fine line. Most customers see the value you and your company bring them. They appreciate your ability to solve their problems and they are willing to pay you for that service. These customers respect you (and the people who work for you) and understand that as a business, you are entitled to a fair profit and will not always be perfect. That doesn't mean they won't push you to perform better or negotiate hard on contracts. Just because a customer is demanding doesn't make him a bad customer.

A few customers will nickel and dime you, run you and your team ragged with service demands that sap your time and your profits, will be late paying bills, and will show you no respect. To keep you on your toes, they will throw your competitors in your face at every turn. Is it really worth it to cater to customers who discount the value you bring to the table by commoditizing your product or service?

While you work hard to give your customers value, do not lose sight of your own. When business relationships are not a win–win, the losing party has a tendency to feel resentful and taken for granted. If your customer feels this way, they usually just walk away. It is a little easier to move on when there is another company with opens arms ready to embrace you.

Walking away from customers is a lot harder. You risk not being able to replace the revenue and you don't want to just give business to a competitor. It took me years to figure out that all customers are not good customers, but once I did, life got so much better. It takes a ton of courage and faith that you and your business will survive.

It is also smart. When you ditch a customer who is sapping your energy and profits, you gain time to spend with your most profitable customers, you become happier and improve your work/life balance, and you free up resources to compete for accounts that will appreciate your value.

If you do decide to break up with a customer, sit down with them first and politely explain why you must end the relationship. You may be surprised that they didn't realize how you felt or the impact they were having on you and your business. In fact, I've found that at least half of the time, we end up negotiating a win–win agreement and the relationship grows stronger.

Accounts Are Lost Most Often Due to Neglect

You don't send me flowers, you don't sing me love songs, you hardly talk to me anymore. Barbara Streisand and Neil Diamond sang these words in their iconic love song "You Don't Bring Me Flowers," where two lovers, who have drifted apart, describe the feeling of being taken for granted. How does it feel to be taken for granted? Can you describe the emotion? Does it make you feel unimportant, small, resentful, angry, and indifferent?

I'd been tapped as the vice president of operations, charged with turning around the worst performing operating group in my company. Things were so bad that the group had delivered negative top line growth for the past 10 years and negative profit growth for the past 5 years. When I took over, the group had a revenue base of $80 million, down from $140 million just a decade earlier.

The situation was unsustainable, but the problem was simple. We were losing customers out the back door faster than we could bring them in the front door. Our competitors, who sensed our growing desperation, were in a feeding frenzy, attacking us from all sides. We had to stop the bleeding or we were doomed.

Structurally, there was nothing wrong with us. We operated within a multibillion-dollar company that had prescribed and proven service delivery processes and systems that worked. In other words, the systems and processes we employed to service our customers were identical to other operating groups that were delivering consistent, sustained success. Our product was high quality and our customers needed our offering. There was no need to rethink, restructure, or redesign the business. Yet customers were leaving us in droves.

The one thing we identified as a problem was that our account managers were not proactively visiting and talking to our customers. Instead they had become reactive to save customers who were terminating contracts and calling in with service issues. Our customers were being neglected. Customers who were not complaining or quitting were being taken for granted.

It took six months to turn things around. We improved our customer retention by 15 points and stopped our downward revenue and profit trends. The solution to our problem and genesis to our turnaround was simple. We shifted our customer engagement from reactive to proactive. Our account managers got focused on systematic customer visitation, calls, and contacts. We turned around 10 years of failure by simply paying attention to our customers.

The reality is most customers are lost because of neglect. They feel taken for granted and unimportant. Often when they defect to a competitor they will list a litany of reasons because it is hard to describe neglect. Neglect happens slowly. It creeps up on customer relationships. It happens because as an account manager, you get into the habit of fighting fires rather than preventing them.

Top account managers set up a system that allows them to fight fires and deal with emergencies *and* proactively engage their customer base. Some set up monthly or quarterly account reviews that focus on account updates and problem solving. Others set aside time each day to reach out to 5 to 10 customers by phone or e-mail. This daily focus is powerful because a handful of contacts each day pays off. Five contacts a day is 25 a week or 100 a month. Those calls and e-mails keep you connected to your clients and let them know you care.

In my experience, a quick phone call check-in goes a long way. I do more business with Sondra, an account manager for a company that sells my company digital advertising, than I do with all of her competitors combined. Her product is not superior—quite honestly, she and all her competitors are about the same. Since we pay by monthly credit card billing, it is easy to forget about our account. Sondra doesn't forget about us, though. She checks in with us every week. Sometimes by phone, other times by e-mail. There is nothing special about what she does. *How are you doing? How can I help you? I have an idea; can we schedule a call? Have a great weekend?* Yet her regular contact ensures that we never forget about her and her company and when we have additional budget to spend on advertising, she always gets it.

Make Breaking Up Hard to Do

One of the Seven Essential Principles of Customer Engagement is: *Customers are people.* They are not companies, objects, things, or a line in your company's financial statement. They are real people—humans with families, motivations, and ambitions. They have feelings and emotions. Most importantly, no matter how much they justify their decisions with logic, those business decisions are made primarily based on emotions.

I believe that with customers, it is important to make business personal. I want to anchor my customers to me emotionally to help them understand the impact that their business has on me personally. I use the *People Love You Levers*, described in detail in Chapter 3, to create this attachment. I do this because I want the thought of breaking up with me to be hard to do.

Despite the cold admonition that "Business is business," the reality is that business is personal. It is personal because people do business with other people. Sure, we all make business decisions that seem impersonal yet, in the moment, emotion still tugs at your heart, causing you to think twice. Sometimes I lose a customer but I want that customer to think twice before they pull the trigger. If it is emotional enough, they may give me a second chance or even tell my competitor to go pound sand. Better yet, when they find that the grass is not greener, they will feel more comfortable coming back.

I believe that we should let customers know how they touch our lives—good and bad. As you connect with customers and build a foundation of trust, tell them the impact their business has on you personally. Let them know how they touch you, your family, and your career. Just as you attempt to step into your customers' shoes to become more empathetic to their situations, help them see the view from your own. This makes their relationship with you even more personal and opens the door to friendship.

When breaking up is hard to do, the ploys and promises made by competitors will not seem so attractive. When there are bumps in the road, you and your customer will be more willing to sit down together and work out solutions. Your value to your customer will extend far beyond a product or service. You will deliver a truly legendary customer experience. And, your relationships with your customers will be deep, profitable, enduring, and virtually unbreakable. Never forget: People don't love your product, company, service, or price. *People Love You.*

Acknowledgments

I've been extraordinarily blessed. It is hard to believe that this is my sixth book—one that I am very passionate about. So many people were willing to sacrifice time to help me build this book and I am eternally grateful. Without you, there would be no *People Love You*.

A heartfelt thank-you to all of the account managers and buyers who sat down with us for interviews; your insights and stories became the heart of the book.

Carrie Blount, thank you, thank you, thank you. I honestly don't know why you put up with me.

Jodi Bagwell, as always you are my compass. Thank you for enduring friendship and encouraging me to stay true to myself.

Lauren Murphy, my wonderful editor, your patience for my perpetual begging for deadline extensions is amazing. Thank you for believing in me and for shepherding this project.

Chris Dods, you have no idea how much I appreciate your coaching and guidance. Thank you for always being there for me.

Jeff Black, thank you very much for taking time out of your very busy schedule to help me shape this book. You are a master at customer relationships.

Mitch Johnson, I love you man. Thank you for coming though for me on this project. You've always been an inspiration to me and I am proud to call you my friend.

Brad Adams thank you for all you do. You are incredible and I am sure I don't tell you this enough.